PATRICK DICKSON

Cape Cod Travel Guide 2023

An Insider's Guide to the Perfect Vacation

Copyright © 2023 by Patrick Dickson

All rights reserved. No part of this publication may be reproduced, stored or transmitted in any form or by any means, electronic, mechanical, photocopying, recording, scanning, or otherwise without written permission from the publisher. It is illegal to copy this book, post it to a website, or distribute it by any other means without permission.

Patrick Dickson asserts the moral right to be identified as the author of this work.

First edition

This book was professionally typeset on Reedsy.
Find out more at reedsy.com

Contents

I   Welcome to Cape Cod

1	Introduction	3
2	Brief History of Cape Cod	7

II   STEPPING INTO CAPE COD

3	Getting to Cape Cod	13
4	Cape Cod Regions	27

III   Top Attractions and Landmarks

5	Cape Cod National Seashore	41
6	Martha's Vineyard	48
7	Nantucket	53
8	Pilgrim Monument	58
9	Cape Cod Rail Trail	61
10	Chatham Lighthouse	65
11	Sandwich Village	70

IV Historic Sites and Museums

12	Plimoth Plantation	77
13	Heritage Museums & Gardens	80
14	Cape Cod Museum of Art	83
15	Edward Gorey House	86
16	Whydah Pirate Museum	89

V Outdoor Dining and Local Cuisine

17	Fresh Seafood and Lobster Shacks	95
18	Farm-to-Table Restaurants	99
19	Local Breweries and Wineries	104
20	Shopping and Entertainment	109

VI SOME PRACTICAL CONSIDERATIONS

21	Accommodation Options	119
22	Practical Information	127

VII Conclusion

I

Welcome to Cape Cod

1

Introduction

Welcome to Cape Cod, a mesmerizing coastal paradise where sandy beaches meet quaint seaside towns, and history merges seamlessly with natural beauty. Nestled along the eastern shores of Massachusetts, Cape Cod is a beloved destination renowned for its captivating landscapes, rich cultural heritage, and a vibrant atmosphere that beckons visitors from around the globe.

In this comprehensive travel guide, we invite you to embark on an extraordinary journey through this enchanting region. Whether you're a first-time visitor or a seasoned explorer, this guide is your ultimate companion, offering valuable insights, expert recommendations, and insider tips to ensure your Cape Cod experience surpasses all expectations.

At the heart of Cape Cod lies a sense of timeless charm and tranquility. As you venture across its sandy shores, breathe in the crisp ocean air, and listen to the soothing sound of waves crashing against the shoreline, you'll feel the weight of the world lift from your shoulders. The natural beauty of Cape Cod is awe-inspiring, with pristine beaches stretching as far as the eye can see, dappled with seashells and the occasional sailboat dotting the horizon.

One of the crown jewels of Cape Cod is the Cape Cod National Seashore, a treasure trove of unspoiled natural wonders. Here, dramatic sand dunes tower above the shoreline, providing a stunning backdrop for exploration. Walk along the miles of pristine trails that wind through the dunes, where you can witness an incredible diversity of plant and animal life, and catch a glimpse of seals basking on the secluded beaches.

Beyond its natural splendor, Cape Cod boasts a rich history that dates back centuries. It was here that the Pilgrims first landed on American soil, marking a pivotal moment in American history. Delve into this captivating past by visiting the iconic Pilgrim Monument, a towering structure that commemorates their arrival and offers breathtaking panoramic views of the Cape's picturesque landscape.

Quaint seaside towns speckle the Cape, each with its own unique character and allure. Explore the colorful streets of Provincetown, a vibrant hub of artistic expression, where galleries, boutiques, and cafes line the bustling Commercial Street. Stroll through the charming village of Chatham, with its picturesque lighthouse and iconic Main Street adorned with charming storefronts. Or meander through the historic streets of Sandwich, where colonial architecture and idyllic gardens transport you to another era.

INTRODUCTION

For those seeking outdoor adventures, Cape Cod offers an array of activities to satiate your wanderlust. Embark on a whale-watching excursion, where you'll witness these majestic creatures breach the surface, leaving you in awe of their grace and power. Set sail on a boat tour to the picturesque islands of Nantucket and Martha's Vineyard, where time seemingly stands still, and idyllic beaches and charming shops await your exploration.

Cape Cod's culinary scene is as delightful as its scenery. Indulge in succulent seafood, freshly caught and expertly prepared, from lobster rolls to clam chowder. Savor farm-to-table cuisine at local restaurants that showcase the region's bountiful harvest of fruits, vegetables, and artisanal products. And no visit to Cape Cod would be complete without sampling the sweet treat that is homemade Cape Cod cranberry ice cream, a local delicacy that will delight your taste buds.

In this guide, we will guide you through the hidden gems, must-visit landmarks, and off-the-beaten-path treasures that define this remarkable destination. From the sun-soaked shores to the captivating history, from the picturesque lighthouses to the vibrant arts scene, our aim is to ensure that your journey through Cape Cod is nothing short of extraordinary.

So, whether you're seeking relaxation on pristine beaches, immersing yourself in the rich history and culture, or indulging in thrilling outdoor adventures, "Cape Cod Travel Guide 2023" is your key to unlocking the true essence of this coastal gem.

So, are you ready to embark on an extraordinary journey through the captivating beauty and rich heritage of Cape Cod? Let "Cape Cod Travel Guide 2023 be your guide, unlocking the secrets and hidden gems that await you on this coastal retreat. It's time to write your own story, create unforgettable memories, and fall in love with the irresistible charm of Cape Cod. Your extraordinary Cape Cod adventure begins here.

2

Brief History of Cape Cod

The history of Cape Cod is a tapestry woven with tales of exploration, settlement, maritime trade, and cultural evolution. From the days of the Native American Wampanoag tribes to the arrival of European settlers and the subsequent development of the region, Cape Cod has witnessed centuries of transformation that have shaped its identity and cultural heritage.

Long before Europeans arrived, Cape Cod was home to the Wampanoag people, who had inhabited the area for thousands of years. They thrived off the bountiful resources of the land and sea, relying on fishing, hunting, and agriculture for sustenance. The Wampanoag tribes had a complex society with a rich oral tradition, and their interactions with early European explorers would profoundly impact their way of life.

The first recorded European encounter with Cape Cod occurred in 1602 when the English explorer Bartholomew Gosnold sailed along the coast. He named the region "Cape Cod" after the abundant codfish he found in the surrounding waters. Gosnold's exploration laid the foundation for future European settlements in the area.

In 1620, the Pilgrims aboard the Mayflower sought religious freedom and a new life in the New World. Originally intending to settle near the mouth of the Hudson River, the ship was blown off course and landed on the tip of Cape Cod. This unplanned arrival led to the signing of the historic Mayflower Compact, a governing document that established the Pilgrims' commitment to self-government. Shortly thereafter, they set foot on Plymouth Rock, marking the beginning of Plymouth Colony, the first permanent European settlement in New England.

Cape Cod played a significant role in the early years of Plymouth Colony. The Pilgrims relied on the resources of the Cape for survival, including its abundant fish, shellfish, and timber. They established trading relationships with the Wampanoag tribes, such as the famous alliance between the Pilgrims and Wampanoag leader Massasoit. This alliance, although complex and at times strained, helped ensure the survival of the Pilgrims and laid the groundwork for future interactions between European settlers and Native American tribes.

As European settlements expanded, Cape Cod became an important center for maritime trade. Its strategic location along the Atlantic Ocean made it a vital hub for fishing, whaling, and shipbuilding. The maritime industry brought wealth and prosperity to the region, attracting merchants and traders from around the world. The town of Provincetown, located at the tip of Cape Cod, became a major port and played a crucial role in the whaling industry during the 19th century.

The 19th century was a time of growth and change for Cape Cod. With the decline of the whaling industry, the focus shifted to tourism and the development of seaside resorts. Wealthy city dwellers sought refuge from urban life in the refreshing ocean breezes and tranquil beaches of Cape Cod. The advent of rail travel in the late 19th century made the region more accessible, further fueling its popularity as a vacation destination.

Cape Cod's natural beauty and cultural charm have attracted numerous artists, writers, and intellectuals over the years. The region became an inspiration for renowned artists such as Edward Hopper, who captured the unique light and serene landscapes of Cape Cod in his paintings. Writers like Henry David Thoreau and Mary Higgins Clark found solace and creative inspiration in the idyllic settings of the Cape.

Today, Cape Cod continues to enchant visitors with its picturesque towns, stunning beaches, and rich history. The Cape Cod National Seashore, established in 1961, preserves much of the region's natural beauty and serves as a testament to its historical and ecological significance. Visitors can explore the iconic lighthouses that dot the coastline, immerse themselves in the region's maritime heritage at museums and historical sites, and engage with the vibrant arts scene that thrives in towns like Provincetown.

Cape Cod's cultural diversity has also evolved over the years. The Cape has seen an influx of Portuguese, Italian, and Irish immigrants, who brought their traditions, customs, and culinary delights, enriching the cultural fabric of the region. Festivals, parades, and local events celebrate this vibrant heritage, offering a glimpse into the diverse tapestry of Cape Cod's population.

In recent decades, Cape Cod has faced challenges associated with rapid development, environmental conservation, and the impact of climate change. Efforts have been made to preserve the region's delicate ecosystems, protect endangered species, and promote sustainable practices. Organizations and initiatives dedicated to preserving Cape Cod's natural beauty and historical heritage are actively engaged in education, conservation, and advocacy.

The history of Cape Cod is a living testament to the resilience and adaptability of its people. From the indigenous tribes who first called this land home to the Pilgrims, mariners, and immigrants who shaped its destiny, Cape Cod's story is one of exploration, survival, and the continuous search for a better life. Today, it stands as a cherished destination that offers visitors a unique blend of natural wonders, cultural heritage, and a sense of tranquility that can only be found in this coastal paradise.

As you embark on your Cape Cod journey, take a moment to reflect on the rich history that surrounds you. Wander the streets of historic towns, visit the museums that bring the past to life, and listen to the stories told by the locals who carry the legacy of their ancestors. By understanding the history of Cape Cod, you'll gain a deeper appreciation for its beauty, its people, and the remarkable journey that has led it to become the beloved destination it is today.

II

STEPPING INTO CAPE COD

3

Getting to Cape Cod

In this chapter, we will explore the different avenues to reach Cape Cod, allowing you to choose the mode of transportation that best suits your needs.

By Air

For those seeking a swift and convenient arrival, several airports serve as gateways to Cape Cod:

Boston Logan International Airport: Situated approximately 70 miles north of Cape Cod, Boston Logan is the primary international airport in the region. Visitors can find numerous domestic and international flights, connecting them to major cities worldwide. From Boston Logan, you have multiple options to reach Cape Cod, including rental cars, private shuttles, or public transportation.

Barnstable Municipal Airport: Located in Hyannis, this regional airport provides a more direct route to Cape Cod. It offers flights from various locations in the United States, making it a convenient choice for travelers who prefer to skip the drive from Boston. Car rentals and taxis are readily available upon arrival.

Tips for Traveling to Cape Cod by Air

1.Check Multiple Airports: Depending on your location and travel plans, consider checking flights to both Boston Logan and Barnstable Municipal Airport. Comparing prices and flight schedules can help you find the most suitable option.

2. Plan Ahead: Cape Cod is a popular destination, especially during the summer months. To secure the best fares and flight options, it is advisable to book your tickets in advance.

3. Consider Layovers: If you have the flexibility, exploring flights with layovers can sometimes lead to significant cost savings. Connecting flights through major hubs can offer more affordable options for reaching Cape Cod.

4. Pack Accordingly: Cape Cod's climate is influenced by its coastal location. Pack layers, including light jackets and sweaters, as temperatures can vary throughout the day. Additionally, don't forget essentials like sunscreen, hats, and comfortable walking shoes for beach strolls and exploring the charming towns.

5. Research Ground Transportation: Before arriving at your chosen airport, familiarize yourself with the ground transportation options available. Whether it's renting a car, booking a shuttle, or using public transportation, having a plan in place will ensure a smooth transition from the airport to your Cape Cod destination.

GETTING TO CAPE COD

By Car:

Driving to Cape Cod allows you the freedom to explore at your own pace and enjoy the scenic beauty along the way. Here are a few options to consider:

From Boston: If you are already in Boston or its surrounding areas, hop onto Interstate 93 South or Route 3 South, which will lead you to the Cape Cod Canal. Cross the canal via the Sagamore or Bourne Bridge, and you will find yourself on Cape Cod's mainland.

From New York City: Take Interstate 95 North until you reach Providence, Rhode Island. From there, follow Route 6 East, also known as the Mid-Cape Highway, which will guide you to Cape Cod's gateway towns.

From other regions: Cape Cod is well-connected to neighboring states via major highways. Consult your GPS or map for the most suitable route from your starting location.

By Bus:

For travelers seeking an affordable and eco-friendly mode of transportation, buses provide a convenient option for reaching Cape Cod. With several bus companies offering routes to the peninsula, you can embark on a comfortable journey while enjoying the scenic beauty along the way. In this section, we will explore the benefits of traveling to Cape Cod by bus and provide useful information to help you plan your trip.

Peter Pan Bus Lines:

Peter Pan Bus Lines is a well-known and reputable bus company that operates from major cities on the East Coast.

With their extensive network, they offer connections to various Cape Cod destinations. Traveling with Peter Pan allows you to enjoy comfortable seating, onboard amenities, and professional drivers who ensure a smooth and pleasant journey.

To reach Cape Cod using Peter Pan Bus Lines, you can consider the following options:

Boston to Cape Cod: If you are starting your journey in Boston, Peter Pan offers multiple daily departures from Boston's South Station to various Cape Cod towns, including Hyannis, Falmouth, and Provincetown. The bus ride typically takes around two to three hours, depending on your destination and traffic conditions.

New York City to Cape Cod: If you are coming from New York City, Peter Pan provides convenient service from the Port Authority Bus Terminal to Cape Cod. Buses run several times a day, allowing you to choose a departure time that suits your schedule. The journey typically takes around five to six hours, depending on traffic.

Plymouth & Brockton Street Railway Co.:

The Plymouth & Brockton Street Railway Co. is another reliable bus company that operates in the Cape Cod region. They offer services connecting Boston, Logan Airport, and other locations to Cape Cod, making it a convenient option for travelers without a car.

Here are some key routes provided by Plymouth & Brockton Street Railway Co.:

Logan Airport to Cape Cod: If you arrive at Logan Airport and want to head directly to Cape Cod, the Plymouth & Brockton Street Railway Co. operates bus services that connect the airport to various Cape Cod towns, including Hyannis, Falmouth, and Provincetown. The buses are scheduled to coincide with flight arrivals, ensuring a smooth transition from the airport to your destination.

Boston to Cape Cod: If you are already in Boston, you can catch a bus from South Station or other designated stops to reach Cape Cod. The Plymouth & Brockton Street Railway Co. offers regular departures throughout the day, allowing flexibility in planning your journey.

Benefits of Traveling to Cape Cod by Bus

Affordability: Bus travel is often more budget-friendly compared to other transportation options. Tickets are typically cheaper than airfare or renting a car, making it an attractive choice for cost-conscious travelers.

1.Scenic Route: Traveling by bus offers the opportunity to admire the beautiful landscapes and coastal views along the way. The journey to Cape Cod takes you through charming New England towns, lush greenery, and glimpses of the sparkling Atlantic Ocean, adding to the overall experience.

2. Environmentally Friendly: Opting for bus travel contributes to reducing carbon emissions, making it a greener choice for eco-conscious travelers.

3. Convenient Schedules: Bus companies like Peter Pan and Plymouth & Brockton offer multiple departure times throughout

the day, providing flexibility in planning your trip. Whether you prefer an early morning departure or a later bus, you can find a schedule that suits your needs.

4. Relaxation and Comfort: Buses are equipped with comfortable seating, ample legroom, and amenities such as onboard Wi-Fi and power outlets. You can sit back, relax, and enjoy the journey while leaving the driving to the professionals.

5. No Parking Hassles: Traveling by bus eliminates the need for parking, especially
if you are visiting Cape Cod without a car. You won't have to worry about finding parking spots or paying parking fees in busy areas. Instead, you can simply hop off the bus and start exploring the attractions and destinations on Cape Cod.

Tips for Traveling to Cape Cod by Bus
1.Plan Your Itinerary: Before embarking on your bus journey, it's helpful to have a rough idea of the towns and attractions you wish to visit on Cape Cod. This will help you choose the most suitable bus route and schedule.

2. Check Timetables and Reservations: Make sure to check the bus schedules and consider making reservations, especially during peak travel periods. This will help secure your seat and ensure a smoother journey.

3. Pack Essentials: Prepare a small bag with essentials for the bus ride, including snacks, water, a book or entertainment, and any necessary travel documents. This will keep you comfortable and entertained throughout the journey.

4. Dress Comfortably: Opt for comfortable clothing and shoes, as you will be spending some time on the bus. Layers are also recommended, as temperatures can vary during the day.

5. Stay Updated: Keep track of any updates or changes to bus schedules, especially if there are any weather conditions or unforeseen circumstances that may affect the service. Stay in touch with the bus company or check their website for real-time information.

6. Connect with Local Transportation: Once you arrive at your destination on Cape Cod, familiarize yourself with the local transportation options, such as public buses or shuttles, to navigate around the towns and explore the attractions further.

By Train:

While there are no direct train services to Cape Cod, incorporating rail travel into your journey can still offer a scenic and enjoyable route to reach this idyllic peninsula. By combining trains with other modes of transportation, you can experience the beauty of the New England landscape and easily access Cape Cod's charming towns. In this section, we will explore the options available for reaching Cape Cod by train and provide useful information to plan your trip.

Amtrak, the national passenger rail service in the United States, offers a convenient way to travel to Cape Cod. Although there is no direct train route to the peninsula, you can take advantage of Amtrak's services to reach nearby cities and then continue your journey by bus, ferry, or car.

Here are some key train routes to consider:

1.Boston: Amtrak provides several daily departures to Boston's South Station from various cities along the East Coast, including New York City, Philadelphia, and Washington, D.C. Once you arrive in Boston, you can easily connect to other transportation options to reach Cape Cod, such as buses, ferries, or rental cars.

2. Providence: If you prefer a more direct route, you can take Amtrak to Providence, Rhode Island. From there, you can rent a car or catch a bus to Cape Cod. The travel time from Providence to Cape Cod is relatively short, making it a convenient option for those seeking a quicker journey.

Connecting with Other Modes of Transportation:
   Once you reach the train station in Boston or Providence, you have various options to continue your journey and reach Cape Cod:
   Rental Cars: Renting a car provides flexibility and freedom to explore Cape Cod at your own pace. Many car rental agencies have locations near train stations, allowing you to easily pick up a vehicle and begin your adventure.

Buses: Bus services like Peter Pan Bus Lines and Plymouth & Brockton Street Railway Co. operate from Boston and Providence to Cape Cod. You can catch a bus from the respective train stations and enjoy a comfortable and affordable ride to your desired destination on the peninsula.

Benefits of Traveling to Cape Cod by Train:
   1.Scenic Landscapes: Train travel allows you to immerse

yourself in the beauty of the New England countryside. As you pass through picturesque towns, rolling hills, and coastal areas, you can witness the charm and natural splendor of the region.

2. Relaxation and Comfort: Trains offer a comfortable and relaxing mode of transportation. You can enjoy spacious seating, ample legroom, and the freedom to move around during the journey. Sit back, relax, and take in the views as you make your way to Cape Cod.

3. Environmental Considerations: Rail travel is an eco-friendly option as it produces fewer carbon emissions compared to other modes of transportation. By choosing the train, you can contribute to sustainable travel and minimize your environmental impact.

4. Convenient Connections: While there is no direct train service to Cape Cod, the convenient connections available at Boston's South Station or Providence allow you to seamlessly continue your journey to the peninsula. With multiple transportation options, you can easily reach your preferred destination on Cape Cod.

5. Relieving Traffic and Parking Concerns: Opting for train travel can alleviate the stress of driving in heavy traffic and finding parking in popular Cape Cod areas. Instead, you can enjoy a relaxed journey and arrive at your destination ready to explore without the hassle of parking or dealing with congested roads.

Tips for Traveling to Cape Cod by Train:

1.Plan your Itinerary: Research and plan your route in advance, considering the train schedules, connections, and the transportation options available from the train stations to your desired destination on Cape Cod.

2. Purchase Tickets in Advance: To secure your seats and ensure a smooth journey, it is advisable to purchase your train tickets in advance. This is especially important during peak travel seasons or holidays when trains can be more crowded.

3. Check Baggage Policies: Familiarize yourself with the baggage policies of the train and any connecting transportation services. Be mindful of size restrictions and consider packing light or opting for easily manageable luggage.

4. Allow for Transit Time: Factor in transit time between train connections and other modes of transportation when planning your itinerary. Leave ample time to comfortably switch between trains, buses, or ferries.

5. Stay Informed: Stay updated with any changes or delays in train schedules. Check the Amtrak website or use their mobile app for real-time updates and notifications about your train's status.

6. Enjoy the Journey: Embrace the unique experience of train travel. Take advantage of the scenic views, relax in the comfortable seating, and engage in activities like reading, listening to music, or enjoying onboard amenities.

By Ferry:

For a unique and scenic mode of transportation to Cape Cod, traveling by ferry is an excellent choice. The ferry services not only offer convenient access to the peninsula but also provide an opportunity to soak in the coastal beauty and enjoy the charm of the surrounding waters.

Steamship Authority:

The Steamship Authority operates ferry services between Cape Cod and the islands of Martha's Vineyard and Nantucket. The ferries depart from various locations and provide a seamless connection between the islands and the mainland.

Here are the key routes provided by the Steamship Authority:

1. Woods Hole to Martha's Vineyard: Ferries depart from Woods Hole, a village in Falmouth, and arrive at either Vineyard Haven or Oak Bluffs on Martha's Vineyard. The journey takes approximately 45 minutes to one hour, depending on the specific route. Once on Martha's Vineyard, you can then access Cape Cod via additional ferry services or bridges.

2. Hyannis to Nantucket: Ferries depart from Hyannis, a town on Cape Cod, and arrive at Nantucket. The journey typically takes around one hour. Hyannis is easily accessible by bus, car, or train, making it a convenient departure point for travelers.

Seastreak:

Seastreak is another ferry operator that offers services between New York City and Cape Cod, with a stop in Martha's Vineyard. This option provides a unique opportunity for those looking to combine a city visit with a Cape Cod adventure.

Here are the key routes provided by Seastreak:

New York City to Cape Cod: Seastreak operates a seasonal ferry service between New York City and Martha's Vineyard, with a stop in Cape Cod. The journey takes approximately five to six hours, providing a leisurely and scenic route to Cape Cod. Once you arrive at Martha's Vineyard, you can access Cape Cod via additional ferry services or bridges.

Benefits of Traveling to Cape Cod by Ferry

1.Scenic Views: Traveling by ferry allows you to admire the stunning coastal landscapes and enjoy panoramic views of the Atlantic Ocean. You can take in the sights, including lighthouses, harbors, and the beauty of the islands, creating a memorable experience.

2. Relaxation and Comfort: Ferries offer comfortable seating and onboard amenities, including refreshments and restrooms. You can unwind, enjoy the gentle sea breeze, and savor the tranquility of the journey.

3. Avoid Traffic: Opting for a ferry ride eliminates the stress of dealing with traffic congestion, especially during peak travel seasons or holidays. You can bypass the busy roads and enjoy a more leisurely and peaceful journey.

4. Accessibility to Islands: Traveling by ferry provides easy access to popular destinations like Martha's Vineyard and Nantucket. You can explore the unique charm, vibrant communities, and scenic beaches of these islands before continuing your adventure on Cape Cod.

Tips for Traveling to Cape Cod by Ferry

1.Check Schedules and Reservations: Ferry services often operate on specific schedules, especially during the peak season. It is advisable to check the ferry company's website or contact them directly to confirm the schedules and make any necessary reservations.

2. Plan Ahead: Ferries can be popular, particularly during the summer months. It is recommended to plan your trip in advance, especially if you have specific dates and times in mind. Early booking ensures you secure your spot and avoids any last-minute disappointments.

3. Parking Considerations: If you plan to bring a vehicle with you on the ferry, make sure to inquire about parking arrangements and fees at the ferry departure point. Some locations may require advanced reservations for parking, so it's important to plan accordingly.

4. Pack Essentials: Prepare a small bag with essentials for your ferry journey, including sunscreen, snacks, water, and any necessary travel documents. It's also a good idea to bring layers of clothing, as temperatures can vary on the water.

5. Be Mindful of Ferry Restrictions: Each ferry service may have specific regulations regarding luggage size, weight limits, and prohibited items. Familiarize yourself with these restrictions to ensure a smooth boarding process.

6. Be Aware of Seasonal Availability: Some ferry services may operate on a seasonal basis, so it's important to check

their schedules and availability for the time of your visit. Plan accordingly and ensure you have alternative transportation options if needed.

7. As Always, Enjoy the Journey: Embrace the maritime adventure and take advantage of the amenities onboard. Relax on the deck, capture photos of the scenic surroundings, or simply enjoy the peacefulness of being on the water.

4

Cape Cod Regions

Upper Cape Cod

Nestled at the southernmost portion of Cape Cod, the region known as Upper Cape Cod serves as the gateway to this picturesque peninsula. Comprising towns such as Falmouth, Sandwich, and Bourne, Upper Cape Cod offers a unique blend of natural beauty, historic charm, and vibrant communities. In this chapter, we will delve into the attractions, activities, and notable restrictions in Upper Cape Cod, providing visitors with valuable insights to enhance their experience.

Falmouth

Falmouth, located on the southwestern coast of Cape Cod, boasts stunning beaches, charming villages, and a rich maritime heritage. Visitors can explore the bustling Main Street with its boutique shops, art galleries, and diverse dining options. Falmouth is also home to the renowned Woods Hole Oceanographic Institution, where visitors can learn about marine science and research.

Restrictions in Falmouth:

1.Beach Regulations: Falmouth's beaches have specific regulations to ensure safety and preservation of the environment. Visitors should adhere to parking restrictions, leash laws for pets, and guidelines for bonfires or grilling.

2. Conservation Areas: Falmouth is known for its beautiful conservation areas, including Beebe Woods and Peterson Farm. Visitors are encouraged to follow trail guidelines, stay on designated paths, and carry out any trash to maintain the pristine nature of these areas.

Sandwich:

As one of the oldest towns on Cape Cod, Sandwich offers a delightful mix of history and natural beauty. Visitors can explore the Sandwich Village, home to historic sites like the Sandwich Glass Museum, the Thornton Burgess Museum, and the Heritage Museums and Gardens, showcasing art, glassware, and the region's heritage.

Restrictions in Sandwich:

1.Historic Sites: While exploring the historic sites in Sandwich, visitors are expected to follow the rules and regulations set by each establishment. These may include restrictions on photography, touching artifacts, and maintaining a respectful demeanor.

2. Beach Parking: If you plan to visit Sandwich's beautiful beaches, be aware of parking restrictions during peak seasons. It

is advisable to arrive early to secure parking spaces, or consider alternative transportation options such as biking or public transportation.

Bourne:
   Located at the Cape Cod Canal's northern entrance, Bourne offers a mix of scenic beauty, outdoor activities, and historical landmarks. Visitors can explore the Cape Cod Canal Visitor Center, where they can learn about the canal's history, enjoy picturesque views, and even spot passing vessels.

Restrictions in Bourne:

1.Cape Cod Canal Regulations: The Cape Cod Canal has specific regulations to ensure the safety of visitors. Fishing, biking, and walking along designated paths are allowed, but swimming, diving, and boat access in certain areas may be restricted. Visitors should familiarize themselves with these guidelines to have a safe and enjoyable experience.

2. Canal Bridges: The Bourne and Sagamore Bridges, which connect Cape Cod to the mainland, may experience heavy traffic during peak travel times. Visitors should plan their journeys accordingly and check for any restrictions or delays that may be in place.

3. COVID-19 Restrictions:
   It's important to note that the COVID-19 pandemic has led to certain restrictions and guidelines to ensure the safety of residents and visitors. As the situation evolves, it is crucial to stay informed about any travel advisories, mask mandates,

capacity limitations, and social distancing measures that may be in effect in Upper Cape Cod. Visitors should check the official websites of the respective towns and the Massachusetts Department of Public Health for the latest information.

Mid Cape Cod

Situated in the middle of Cape Cod, the region known as Mid Cape Cod is a vibrant and bustling area that offers a perfect balance of natural beauty, cultural attractions, and recreational opportunities. Comprised of towns such as Barnstable, Hyannis, and Yarmouth, Mid Cape Cod serves as a central hub for visitors looking to explore the peninsula. Here we will delve into the attractions, activities, and notable highlights of Mid Cape Cod, providing valuable insights to enhance your experience.

Hyannis:

As the largest village in the town of Barnstable, Hyannis is often considered the commercial and transportation hub of Cape Cod. It offers a diverse range of attractions, from pristine beaches to vibrant shopping districts and cultural landmarks. Hyannis is also famous as the hometown of the Kennedy family, and visitors can explore the John F. Kennedy Hyannis Museum to learn about the family's legacy.

Highlights of Hyannis:

1.Main Street: Hyannis's Main Street is a vibrant hub of activity, featuring an array of shops, boutiques, art galleries, and restaurants. Visitors can stroll along the street, enjoy local cuisine, and find unique souvenirs.

2.;Hyannis Harbor: The picturesque Hyannis Harbor is a focal point of the village. From here, visitors can embark on harbor cruises, fishing charters, and ferries to nearby islands such as Nantucket and Martha's Vineyard.

3. Kalmus Beach: Located on the south side of Hyannis, Kalmus Beach is a popular spot for windsurfing and kiteboarding due to its favorable wind conditions. Visitors can also relax on the sandy beach and take in views of Nantucket Sound.

Barnstable:
   As the largest town on Cape Cod, Barnstable encompasses several villages, each with its unique character and attractions. The town offers a mix of historic landmarks, scenic vistas, and cultural venues, making it an ideal destination for exploration.

Highlights of Barnstable:
   1.Barnstable Village: Barnstable Village is the historic center of the town, featuring charming colonial architecture, boutique shops, and art galleries. Visitors can also explore the Barnstable Historical Society and the Sturgis Library, which is the oldest library building in the United States.

2. Sandy Neck Beach: Located in the village of West Barnstable, Sandy Neck Beach offers a breathtaking stretch of shoreline, dunes, and marshlands. It is a popular spot for swimming, hiking, birdwatching, and off-road vehicle adventures.

Yarmouth:
   Yarmouth, located on the north side of Mid Cape Cod, combines scenic beauty, family-friendly attractions, and a lively atmosphere. It offers a range of activities for all ages, from

serene beaches to amusement parks and golf courses.

Highlights of Yarmouth include:

1.Seagull Beach: With its calm waters, soft sand, and ample parking, Seagull Beach is a favorite among families. It features picnic areas, restrooms, and lifeguards on duty, providing a safe and enjoyable beach experience.

2.;Cape Cod Inflatable Park: The Cape Cod Inflatable Park in West Yarmouth is a thrilling amusement park that offers an array of inflatable rides and attractions. From towering water slides to obstacle courses, visitors of all ages can enjoy a day of fun and excitement.

3. Bass River: Bass River, which flows through Yarmouth, provides opportunities for boating, kayaking, and fishing. It is a scenic waterway with picturesque views and serene surroundings.

Lower Cape Cod

Nestled at the easternmost tip of Cape Cod, the region known as Lower Cape Cod offers a tranquil escape from the bustling crowds and showcases the natural beauty of the outer cape. Comprising towns such as Chatham, Orleans, and Wellfleet, Lower Cape Cod captivates visitors with its pristine beaches, charming villages, and rich maritime history.

Chatham:

Chatham, known for its picturesque Main Street and quintessential Cape Cod charm, is a must-visit destination in Lower Cape Cod. This seaside town exudes elegance and offers a blend of historic landmarks, stunning beaches, and vibrant shops and galleries.

Highlights of Chatham:

11.Lighthouse Beach: Lighthouse Beach is one of Chatham's most iconic attractions, featuring the Chatham Lighthouse and the expansive sandy shoreline. Visitors can enjoy scenic walks along the beach, observe the lighthouse, and soak in the serene beauty of the Atlantic Ocean.

2. Chatham Fish Pier: The Chatham Fish Pier provides a glimpse into the region's rich fishing heritage. Visitors can witness local fishermen unloading their catches, purchase fresh seafood, or even embark on a fishing charter to experience the thrill of deep-sea fishing.

3. Main Street: Chatham's Main Street is lined with historic homes, boutique shops, art galleries, and renowned restaurants. It's a delightful place to stroll, shop for unique souvenirs, and savor local cuisine.

Orleans:

Situated in the middle of Lower Cape Cod, Orleans offers a harmonious blend of natural beauty and cultural attractions. The town boasts picturesque beaches, pristine nature trails, and a vibrant downtown area.

Highlights of Orleans include:

1.Nauset Beach: Nauset Beach is a stunning ocean beach

renowned for its rolling sand dunes and powerful surf. Visitors can swim, sunbathe, or simply enjoy a leisurely stroll along the shoreline.

2. Cape Cod National Seashore: A significant portion of the Cape Cod National Seashore is located in Orleans. The pristine landscapes, walking trails, and scenic vistas offer ample opportunities for outdoor exploration and appreciation of the area's natural beauty.

3. Main Street: Orleans' Main Street is lined with charming boutiques, antique shops, and art galleries. Visitors can browse unique items, explore local crafts, and indulge in delicious seafood and homemade ice cream.

Wellfleet:

Wellfleet, located on the outermost edge of Cape Cod, is known for its stunning beaches, picturesque harbor, and thriving arts scene. This quaint town offers a perfect blend of natural beauty, history, and cultural experiences.

Highlights of Wellfleet include:

1.Marconi Beach: Marconi Beach is part of the Cape Cod National Seashore and is known for its towering sand dunes and pristine shoreline. It's a popular spot for swimming, surfing, and picnicking, and visitors can also explore the Marconi Station Site, which played a significant role in the history of wireless communication.

2. Wellfleet Harbor: Wellfleet Harbor is a picturesque waterfront

area dotted with fishing boats, sailboats, and charming seafood shacks. Visitors can indulge in fresh seafood delicacies, embark on a harbor cruise, or simply enjoy the scenic beauty of the harbor.

3. Wellfleet Bay Wildlife Sanctuary: Nature enthusiasts will appreciate the Wellfleet Bay Wildlife Sanctuary, which spans over 1,100 acres of salt marshes, woodlands, and beaches. The sanctuary offers walking trails, birdwatching opportunities, and educational programs that highlight the diverse wildlife and ecosystems of Cape Cod.

Outer Cape Cod

Nestled at the outermost tip of Cape Cod, the region known as Outer Cape Cod offers a breathtaking and untamed landscape that captivates visitors with its pristine beaches, picturesque dunes, and rich natural beauty. Comprising towns such as Provincetown, Truro, and Wellfleet, Outer Cape Cod beckons with its secluded charm, artistic heritage, and outdoor adventures.

Provincetown:

Provincetown, fondly referred to as "P-Town," is a vibrant and eclectic town that embraces its reputation as an artistic and cultural haven. Known for its thriving LGBTQ+ community, Provincetown offers a lively atmosphere, stunning beaches, and a rich history.

Highlights of Provincetown include;

1.Commercial Street: Commercial Street is the heartbeat of

Provincetown, featuring an array of art galleries, boutique shops, restaurants, and entertainment venues. Visitors can immerse themselves in the town's vibrant energy, enjoy street performances, and explore unique shops.

2. Race Point Beach: Race Point Beach, located within the Cape Cod National Seashore, is a pristine stretch of sand that offers stunning views of the Atlantic Ocean. Visitors can swim, sunbathe, or take leisurely walks along the shoreline.

3. Pilgrim Monument: The iconic Pilgrim Monument, towering over Provincetown, commemorates the arrival of the Pilgrims in 1620. Visitors can climb to the top of the monument for panoramic views of the town and its surrounding natural beauty.

Truro:

Truro, situated between Provincetown and Wellfleet, is renowned for its unspoiled natural beauty, charming rural character, and serene beaches. The town offers a peaceful retreat for nature lovers and those seeking tranquility.

Highlights of Truro include:

1.Cape Cod National Seashore: A significant portion of the Cape Cod National Seashore is located in Truro, offering vast stretches of sandy beaches, rolling sand dunes, and picturesque trails. Visitors can explore the diverse ecosystems, enjoy birdwatching, or simply relax in the pristine surroundings.

2. Highland Light: The Highland Light, also known as Cape Cod Light, is a historic lighthouse that stands proudly on the

bluffs of Truro. Visitors can take guided tours to learn about its fascinating history and enjoy panoramic views of the coastline.

3. Wellfleet Bay Wildlife Sanctuary: Although part of Wellfleet, the Wellfleet Bay Wildlife Sanctuary extends into Truro. This sanctuary encompasses salt marshes, woodlands, and tidal flats, providing ample opportunities for nature exploration, birdwatching, and educational programs.

Wellfleet:

Wellfleet, known for its charming harbor, picturesque beaches, and artistic heritage, offers a perfect blend of natural beauty, cultural experiences, and culinary delights. The town's unspoiled landscapes and thriving arts scene attract visitors from near and far.

Highlights of Wellfleet include;

1.Wellfleet Harbor: Wellfleet Harbor is a picturesque waterfront area dotted with fishing boats, sailboats, and charming seafood shacks. Visitors can indulge in fresh seafood delicacies, embark on a harbor cruise, or simply enjoy the scenic beauty of the harbor.

2. Marconi Beach: Marconi Beach, located within the Cape Cod National Seashore, is famous for its towering sand dunes and pristine shoreline. It's a popular spot for swimming, surfing, and picnicking, and visitors can also explore the Marconi Station Site, which played a significant role in the history of wireless communication.

3. Wellfleet Bay Wildlife Sanctuary

Outer Beaches

Outer Cape Cod is renowned for its stunning and secluded beaches that showcase the untamed beauty of the Atlantic Ocean. From the wide sandy shores of Race Point Beach in Provincetown to the breathtaking dunes of Head of the Meadow Beach in Truro, visitors can immerse themselves in the serenity and tranquility of these natural wonders.

Hiking and Biking Trails: Outer Cape Cod is a paradise for outdoor enthusiasts, offering an extensive network of hiking and biking trails that wind through scenic landscapes and showcase the region's diverse flora and fauna. The Province Lands Trail System in Provincetown and the Head of the Meadow Trail in Truro are popular choices for nature lovers.

Artistic and Cultural Heritage: Outer Cape Cod has long been a haven for artists and creatives. Provincetown, in particular, is known for its thriving arts scene, with numerous galleries, studios, and theaters showcasing the works of local and internationally renowned artists. Visitors can explore art exhibits, attend performances, and immerse themselves in the vibrant creative energy of the town.

Whale Watching: The waters off the coast of Outer Cape Cod are home to a rich marine ecosystem, and visitors have the opportunity to embark on thrilling whale watching excursions. From Provincetown and other nearby ports, you can witness the majestic humpback, fin, and minke whales as they breach and play in their natural habitat.

III

Top Attractions and Landmarks

While we have touched briefly on some of these top attractions and Landmarks in the previous chapter, we will be giving you some more details in this part of the book.

5

Cape Cod National Seashore

Cape Cod National Seashore is a must-visit destination for nature enthusiasts and beach lovers. Located on the eastern coast of Massachusetts, Cape Cod National Seashore is a 40-mile stretch of pristine beaches, sand dunes, marshes, and forests that offer visitors a unique experience of natural beauty and serenity.

Cape Cod National Seashore was established in 1961, after a decade-long campaign by environmentalists and conservationists to protect the unique natural features of Cape Cod from commercial development. The area had been inhabited by Native American tribes for thousands of years before European settlers arrived in the 17th century. The seashore area was later used for farming, fishing, and whaling, before becoming a popular tourist destination in the 20th century.

The seashore's main attraction is its pristine beaches, which offer visitors a chance to relax, swim, sunbathe, and enjoy various water activities. Some of the popular beaches in Cape

Cod National Seashore include Coast Guard Beach, Nauset Light Beach, Marconi Beach, and Head of the Meadow Beach. These beaches have been consistently ranked among the best beaches in the United States by various travel publications.

Trails and Hiking:

Cape Cod National Seashore has an extensive network of hiking and biking trails that allow visitors to explore the diverse landscape and ecosystem of the seashore. Some of the popular hiking trails include the Great Island Trail, the Nauset Marsh Trail, and the Atlantic White Cedar Swamp Trail. These trails offer stunning views of the beaches, marshes, ponds, and forests, as well as opportunities for wildlife watching and birding.

Cultural Landmarks

Cape Cod National Seashore is also home to several cultural landmarks that provide visitors with a glimpse into the seashore's history and heritage. Some of the notable landmarks include the Highland Light, a historic lighthouse built in 1857; the Marconi Station Site, where the first transatlantic wireless communication took place in 1903; and the Salt Pond Visitor Center, which houses exhibits and educational programs on the seashore's natural and cultural history.

Wildlife

Cape Cod National Seashore is home to a diverse range of wildlife, including several species of birds, mammals, and marine life. Visitors can spot seals, whales, dolphins, and various species of seabirds along the seashore's beaches and offshore waters. The seashore is also home to several species of freshwater and saltwater fish, as well as endangered species like the piping plover, the roseate tern, and the North Atlantic right whale.

Visitor Centers

Cape Cod National Seashore has three visitor centers located in Eastham, Provincetown, and Wellfleet. These visitor centers offer a range of services and amenities to visitors, including maps, exhibits, educational programs, and ranger-led tours. Visitors can learn about the seashore's natural and cultural history, as well as get advice on hiking, biking, and other activities.

Provincetown

Provincetown, located at the northern tip of Cape Cod in Massachusetts, is a vibrant and unique destination that attracts visitors from around the world. With its rich history, diverse culture, beautiful beaches, and thriving arts scene, Provincetown offers a little something for everyone.

Provincetown has a fascinating history that dates back to the arrival of the Pilgrims in 1620. The Mayflower Compact, one of the first governing documents of the New World, was signed in Provincetown Harbor. The town's maritime heritage is evident in its historic architecture, including the iconic Pilgrim Monument, a towering granite structure that commemorates the Pilgrims' arrival.

Provincetown has long been a haven for artists and creative minds. It is renowned as an arts colony and continues to inspire painters, writers, actors, and musicians. The town is dotted with art galleries, showcasing a wide range of contemporary and traditional artwork. The Provincetown Art Association and Museum is a must-visit for art enthusiasts, featuring a diverse collection of local and international works.

Theater enthusiasts will find a thriving performing arts scene in Provincetown. The Provincetown Theater hosts a variety of productions throughout the year, ranging from classic plays to experimental works. The town is also famous for its annual Provincetown Tennessee Williams Theater Festival, celebrating the works of the renowned American playwright.

The heart and soul of Provincetown is Commercial Street, a bustling thoroughfare that runs parallel to the harbor. Lined with colorful storefronts, art galleries, restaurants, and bars, Commercial Street exudes a vibrant and welcoming atmosphere. It is the perfect place to explore, shop for unique souvenirs, savor delicious seafood, and experience the town's lively energy.

Provincetown Harbor

Provincetown Harbor is not only historically significant but also offers breathtaking natural beauty. The harbor is a bustling hub of activity, with fishing boats, pleasure crafts, and ferry services transporting visitors to and from Boston and other nearby islands. Visitors can take a scenic harbor cruise or embark on a whale watching excursion to witness the majestic creatures that frequent the waters off Provincetown.

Beaches:

Provincetown is home to some of the most picturesque beaches on Cape Cod. Herring Cove Beach and Race Point

Beach are popular choices, offering expansive sandy shores, stunning dunes, and breathtaking sunsets. These beaches are perfect for swimming, sunbathing, picnicking, and long walks along the shoreline. Visitors can also explore the Province Lands, a unique natural landscape characterized by sand dunes, heathlands, and coastal forests.

Provincetown Museum:

The Provincetown Museum, located near the Pilgrim Monument, is a fantastic place to learn about the town's history and heritage. The museum showcases exhibits that cover a wide range of topics, including the Mayflower Compact, the town's maritime history, the art colony, and the LGBTQ+ community's influence on Provincetown. It provides a comprehensive and engaging exploration of Provincetown's past and present.

LGBTQ+ Destination:

Provincetown has gained recognition as one of the most LGBTQ+-friendly destinations in the United States. The town has a long history of welcoming the LGBTQ+ community, and today it hosts an annual LGBTQ+ Pride celebration that attracts thousands of visitors. Commercial Street is dotted with LGBTQ+-owned businesses, clubs, and bars, creating a vibrant and inclusive atmosphere that celebrates diversity and acceptance.

Provincetown Film Festival:

Film enthusiasts will appreciate Provincetown's vibrant arts scene extends to the realm of film with the Provincetown Film Festival. This annual event, held in June, showcases a diverse range of independent films, documentaries, and shorts from both established and emerging filmmakers. The festival attracts renowned actors, directors, and industry professionals, creating an exciting and dynamic atmosphere for film lovers.

During the festival, screenings take place in various venues across Provincetown, including the historic Art Deco-style Provincetown Town Hall and the Waters Edge Cinema. In addition to film screenings, the festival also features panel discussions, Q&A sessions with filmmakers, and special events that provide insights into the world of cinema.

The Provincetown Film Festival is known for its inclusive and progressive programming, highlighting stories and perspectives from underrepresented communities. It often showcases films that explore LGBTQ+ themes, social justice issues, and unique perspectives on identity and culture.

One of the festival's highlights is the presentation of awards to outstanding films and filmmakers. The festival jury recognizes achievements in categories such as Best Narrative Feature, Best Documentary Feature, and Best Short Film, among others. These awards contribute to the festival's reputation for celebrating artistic excellence and pushing the boundaries of independent filmmaking.

Beyond the festival, Provincetown continues to embrace the cinematic arts throughout the year. The Waters Edge Cinema, operated by the Provincetown Film Society, screens a diverse selection of independent and foreign films, providing year-round entertainment for film enthusiasts.

In addition to the film festival, Provincetown hosts other cultural events that showcase the town's creative spirit. The Provincetown Tennessee Williams Theater Festival, mentioned earlier, features performances of the renowned playwright's works in various venues throughout the town. The event attracts theater enthusiasts and lovers of Williams' plays from all over.

Provincetown also boasts a thriving live performance scene, with theaters and cabaret venues hosting a range of shows, including comedy acts, musical performances, and drag shows. The town's vibrant nightlife contributes to its reputation as a hub for artistic expression and entertainment.

6

Martha's Vineyard

Martha's Vineyard, an idyllic island off the coast of Massachusetts, is renowned for its natural beauty, charming towns, and rich history. With its pristine beaches, picturesque landscapes, and a vibrant cultural scene, Martha's Vineyard has become a popular destination for travelers seeking a unique and memorable experience. Here, we will explore the attractions, landmarks, and highlights of Martha's Vineyard, showcasing why it is a must-visit destination.

Martha's Vineyard is located about seven miles off the coast of Cape Cod and spans approximately 100 square miles. The island consists of six towns: Edgartown, Oak Bluffs, Vineyard Haven, West Tisbury, Chilmark, and Aquinnah. Each town has its distinct character and offers visitors a diverse range of attractions and activities.

Beaches

Martha's Vineyard is renowned for its stunning beaches that

offer visitors the perfect opportunity to relax, swim, and soak up the sun. Some of the most popular beaches include South Beach in Edgartown, State Beach that stretches between Oak Bluffs and Edgartown, and Menemsha Beach in Chilmark. These beaches boast pristine sands, clear waters, and breathtaking views, making them ideal for both relaxation and water activities.

Lighthouses:

The island is dotted with picturesque lighthouses that add to its coastal charm. One of the most iconic lighthouses is the Edgartown Lighthouse, which stands proudly at the entrance of the harbor and offers panoramic views of the town and the sea. The Gay Head Lighthouse in Aquinnah is another notable landmark, perched atop the colorful clay cliffs and providing stunning vistas of the Atlantic Ocean.

Aquinnah Cliffs:

Speaking of Aquinnah, this town is also home to the dramatic Aquinnah Cliffs, also known as the Gay Head Cliffs. These magnificent clay cliffs are a unique geological formation that showcases vibrant layers of red, orange, and white. Visitors can enjoy breathtaking views of the cliffs and the surrounding landscape from the observation decks and walking trails.

Gingerbread Cottages:

Oak Bluffs is famous for its whimsical and colorful Gingerbread Cottages. These charming, Victorian-style cottages feature ornate details, vibrant paint colors, and intricate architectural designs. Walking through the Cottage City Historic District feels like stepping into a fairytale village, with the cottages exuding a sense of enchantment and nostalgia.

Martha's Vineyard Camp Meeting Association:

While in Oak Bluffs, visitors should explore the Martha's Vineyard Camp Meeting Association (MVCMA). This historic community dates back to the 19th century and features a collection of charming Victorian cottages arranged in a circular pattern around a central park known as the Tabernacle. The Tabernacle is a focal point for religious services, concerts, and community events.

Cultural and Arts Scene:

Martha's Vineyard is known for its thriving arts and cultural scene. The island hosts numerous art galleries, showcasing a variety of works from local and internationally renowned artists. The Martha's Vineyard Museum in Vineyard Haven offers a glimpse into the island's rich history and heritage through its exhibits and collections.

The island also boasts a vibrant theater scene, with the Martha's Vineyard Playhouse in Vineyard Haven staging a diverse range of performances, including plays, musicals, and readings. The summer season brings the Martha's Vineyard Film Festival, featuring screenings of independent films and thought-provoking documentaries.

Farmers Markets and Farm-to-Table Cuisine:

Martha's Vineyard is home to several farmers markets, where visitors can explore a variety of local produce, artisanal goods, and crafts. The West Tisbury Farmers Market, held in the charming town center, is a popular destination for fresh fruits, vegetables, homemade baked goods, and handmade crafts. The farmers markets provide an opportunity to connect with local farmers and artisans while enjoying the vibrant atmosphere.

In addition to the farmers markets, Martha's Vineyard offers a thriving farm-to-table culinary scene. Many restaurants on the island prioritize using locally sourced ingredients, showcasing the abundance of fresh seafood, organic produce, and artisanal products available. Visitors can indulge in delicious meals that highlight the island's unique flavors and culinary traditions.

Chappaquiddick Island:
Connected to Martha's Vineyard by a small ferry, Chappaquiddick Island offers a quieter and more secluded experience. The island is home to pristine beaches, serene nature reserves, and the Mytoi Japanese Garden, a hidden gem featuring peaceful ponds, winding paths, and beautiful flora.

Biking and Outdoor Activities:

Martha's Vineyard is a paradise for outdoor enthusiasts, with an extensive network of biking trails that allow visitors to explore the island's natural beauty at their own pace. The Martha's Vineyard Bike Path spans more than 40 miles and takes riders through picturesque landscapes, charming towns, and scenic vistas. Biking is an excellent way to visit the island's attractions and enjoy the fresh sea breeze.

For those who prefer hiking, the Manuel F. Correllus State Forest in West Tisbury offers miles of trails winding through oak and pine forests. The forest is also a haven for birdwatching and wildlife spotting, making it a favorite destination for nature lovers.

Martha's Vineyard Agricultural Fair:

Every August, Martha's Vineyard hosts the Martha's Vineyard Agricultural Fair, a cherished annual event that celebrates the island's agricultural heritage and community spirit. The fair features livestock shows, crafts, games, agricultural displays, and live entertainment, providing a fun-filled experience for visitors of all ages.

Transportation:

Getting to Martha's Vineyard is part of the adventure, as most visitors arrive by ferry from Cape Cod. The ferry ride itself offers beautiful views of the coastline and the opportunity to spot marine life. Once on the island, transportation options include rental cars, bicycles, taxis, and public transportation, making it easy to navigate and explore the various towns and attractions.

7

Nantucket

Nantucket, a picturesque island off the coast of Massachusetts, is a destination that embodies charm, history, and natural beauty. Known for its cobblestone streets, iconic lighthouses, and historic homes, Nantucket offers a quintessential New England experience.

Nantucket offers a quintessential New England experience. In this article, we will delve into the attractions, landmarks, and highlights of Nantucket, showcasing why it is a must-visit destination.

Nantucket has a rich maritime history that dates back to the early 18th century. Once a prominent whaling hub, the island's historic district is filled with beautifully preserved homes and buildings from the whaling era. The cobblestone streets, white picket fences, and weathered gray shingles add to the island's nostalgic charm. Exploring the historic district, visitors will find the Whaling Museum, which provides insights into Nantucket's whaling heritage through exhibits, artifacts, and interactive displays.

Beaches:

Nantucket is renowned for its pristine beaches, boasting soft sand and crystal-clear waters. Some of the island's popular beaches include Surfside Beach, which offers excellent surfing conditions, Madaket Beach with its stunning sunsets, and Cisco Beach, known for its expansive shoreline and picturesque dunes. These beaches provide an ideal setting for swimming, sunbathing, beachcombing, and picnicking.

Sankaty Head Lighthouse:

One of Nantucket's most iconic landmarks is the Sankaty Head Lighthouse. Located in the village of Siasconset, this striking red and white lighthouse stands atop a bluff, offering panoramic views of the Atlantic Ocean. Visitors can take a guided tour to learn about the lighthouse's history and enjoy the breathtaking coastal scenery. The area surrounding the lighthouse is also a popular spot for coastal walks and birdwatching.

Brant Point Lighthouse:

Another notable lighthouse on the island is Brant Point Lighthouse, situated at the entrance of Nantucket Harbor. It is one of the oldest lighthouses in the United States and serves as a welcoming beacon for boats entering the harbor. Visitors can stroll along the waterfront promenade and admire the lighthouse's classic design while taking in the scenic harbor views.

Great Point Lighthouse:

For those seeking a more adventurous experience, a visit to

Great Point Lighthouse is a must. Located at the northeastern tip of Nantucket, Great Point Lighthouse can be reached by driving along the pristine beaches of Coskata-Coatue Wildlife Refuge or by taking a guided tour. The journey to the lighthouse offers opportunities for wildlife spotting, as seals, shorebirds, and even the occasional deer can be seen along the way.

The town of Nantucket is a charming and vibrant center filled with boutique shops, art galleries, and restaurants. The cobblestone streets are lined with historic homes, many of which have been converted into stylish inns and bed-and-breakfast establishments. Main Street is the heart of the town, offering an array of shops selling unique clothing, jewelry, and gifts. The Wharf area is bustling with activity, with fishing boats, yachts, and ferries coming and going from the island.

Nantucket Whaling Museum:

For history buffs, the Nantucket Whaling Museum is a fascinating place to explore. The museum showcases Nantucket's whaling history through exhibits that include whaling artifacts, models of whaling ships, and interactive displays. Visitors can learn about the island's role in the whaling industry and gain insight into the lives of the brave men and women who ventured out to sea in search of whales.

Cycling and Nature:

Nantucket is a cyclist's paradise, with over 30 miles of bike paths that traverse the island's scenic landscapes.

Cycling is a popular way to explore Nantucket, allowing visitors to enjoy the island's natural beauty at a leisurely pace. The bike paths wind through picturesque coastal areas, meadows, and forests, offering stunning views along the way. Bicycles can be rented from various rental shops in town, making it convenient for visitors to embark on their cycling adventures.

Coskata-Coatue Wildlife Refuge:

The Coskata-Coatue Wildlife Refuge is a pristine conservation area located on the northeastern part of Nantucket. This protected refuge is home to a diverse range of plant and animal species and offers visitors the opportunity to explore its beautiful landscapes. Guided tours are available, allowing visitors to learn about the local flora and fauna while enjoying the scenic beauty of the refuge.

Nantucket Whaling History Trail:

For those interested in delving deeper into Nantucket's whaling history, the Nantucket Whaling History Trail is a fascinating self-guided tour. This trail takes visitors to significant historical sites related to the island's whaling industry, including the Old North Vestry, the African Meeting House, and the Hadwen & Barney Candle Factory. Along the trail, informative plaques provide insights into the island's whaling heritage, allowing visitors to envision the bustling whaling port that Nantucket once was.

Eateries and Culinary Delights:

Nantucket is renowned for its culinary scene, offering a wide array of dining options to satisfy every palate. From fresh seafood and New England clam chowder to gourmet cuisine and farm-to-table delights, the island's restaurants and eateries showcase the finest local ingredients. Visitors can indulge in delicious lobster rolls, sample freshly shucked oysters, or savor delectable dishes crafted by talented chefs. Nantucket also hosts the Nantucket Food and Wine Festival, an annual event that celebrates the island's culinary excellence with tastings, cooking demonstrations, and wine pairings.

Annual Events:

Throughout the year, Nantucket hosts a variety of events and festivals that add to its vibrant atmosphere. The Nantucket Daffodil Festival, held in April, welcomes spring with colorful daffodil displays, parades, and activities for the whole family. The Nantucket Wine Festival, mentioned earlier, attracts wine enthusiasts from around the world who come to indulge in tastings, seminars, and exclusive events. Other events include the Nantucket Film Festival, featuring independent films and screenings, and the Nantucket Christmas Stroll, a festive holiday celebration with carolers, decorations, and local vendors.

8

Pilgrim Monument

The Pilgrim Monument, located in Provincetown, Massachusetts, stands as a towering tribute to the arrival of the Pilgrims and their significant role in American history. This iconic monument serves as a symbol of freedom, resilience, and the pursuit of a new beginning.

The Pilgrim Monument commemorates the first landing of the Pilgrims in Provincetown in 1620, prior to their settlement in Plymouth. This historic event marked the beginning of the Pilgrims' journey to establish a society based on religious freedom and the principles of self-governance. The monument honors the Pilgrims' courage, determination, and enduring impact on the development of the United States.

The idea for the Pilgrim Monument was conceived in the late 19th century, when a group of citizens sought to create a monument to honor the Pilgrims. The cornerstone was laid in 1907, and the monument was completed in 1910. Designed by architect Willard T. Sears, the monument stands at an impressive height of 252 feet and is made of granite sourced from Stonington, Maine.

Architecture and Symbolism:

The Pilgrim Monument exhibits a blend of architectural styles, including Renaissance Revival and Gothic Revival elements. Its intricate design features a square base that transitions into an octagonal tower, topped by an observation deck and a prominent crowning feature known as the "Crown." The Crown, reminiscent of a lantern, is adorned with a weather vane symbolizing the Mayflower.

Visitors can ascend the monument's 116 steps and take an elevator to the observation deck, which offers panoramic views of Provincetown, Cape Cod, and the surrounding Atlantic Ocean. On a clear day, the vista extends for miles, providing a breathtaking vantage point to appreciate the natural beauty of the area.

Provincetown Museum:

Adjacent to the Pilgrim Monument is the Provincetown Museum, which provides visitors with a deeper understanding of the Pilgrims' journey, the history of Provincetown, and the cultural heritage of the region. The museum features exhibits that showcase artifacts, documents, and interactive displays, allowing visitors to explore the Pilgrims' story, the town's maritime history, and the vibrant arts community that thrives in Provincetown.

Mayflower Compact:

One of the significant documents in American history, the

Mayflower Compact, is closely associated with the Pilgrims' arrival in Provincetown. The compact, signed by the Pilgrims aboard the Mayflower, served as a governing agreement for the newly established Plymouth Colony. A replica of the Mayflower Compact is on display at the Provincetown Museum, allowing visitors to view this historic document that laid the foundation for democratic governance in the United States.

Pilgrim Monument and Provincetown Museum Gardens:

The grounds surrounding the Pilgrim Monument and the Provincetown Museum are beautifully landscaped with gardens that enhance the visitor experience. The gardens feature native plant species, including roses, hydrangeas, and various perennials. Walking through the gardens provides a serene and tranquil atmosphere, where visitors can reflect on the history and significance of the monument.

Annual Events and Festivals:

The Pilgrim Monument and Provincetown Museum also play host to a variety of events and festivals throughout the year. The annual lighting of the monument during the holiday season is a cherished tradition that brings the community together. Other events include lectures, concerts, art exhibitions, and historical reenactments, offering visitors opportunities to engage with the cultural and artistic heritage of Provincetown.

9

Cape Cod Rail Trail

The Cape Cod Rail Trail, stretching for 27 miles along the scenic Cape Cod peninsula in Massachusetts, is a beloved recreational pathway that offers locals and visitors alike an opportunity to explore the region's natural beauty and rich history. This popular trail follows the route of the former Old Colony Railroad, providing a unique and accessible way to experience Cape Cod's diverse landscapes, charming towns, and coastal treasures.

The Cape Cod Rail Trail traces its roots back to the early 19th century when the Old Colony Railroad operated a railway line connecting Cape Cod to Boston and other parts of Massachusetts. However, as the popularity of rail travel declined, the railway was abandoned in the mid-20th century. In the late 1970s, the idea of transforming the railway corridor into a recreational trail gained traction, and the Cape Cod Rail Trail was officially established in 1979.

Trail Route and Highlights:

The Cape Cod Rail Trail begins in South Dennis and winds its way through picturesque Cape Cod towns, including Harwich, Brewster, Orleans, Eastham, and Wellfleet, before reaching its endpoint in South Wellfleet. The trail offers a diverse range of scenic landscapes, including forests, marshes, ponds, and coastal vistas, allowing users to immerse themselves in Cape Cod's natural beauty.

One of the highlights of the trail is the Nickerson State Park in Brewster, where users can take a detour and explore its expansive network of trails, freshwater ponds, and serene woodlands. The park offers opportunities for swimming, picnicking, fishing, and camping, providing a perfect spot for relaxation and outdoor recreation.

Another notable feature along the trail is the Salt Pond Visitor Center in Eastham, which is part of the Cape Cod National Seashore. The visitor center provides valuable information about the natural and cultural history of Cape Cod, and visitors can learn about the region's unique coastal ecosystems, wildlife, and conservation efforts.

Scenic Beauty and Wildlife:

As users traverse the Cape Cod Rail Trail, they are treated to breathtaking views of Cape Cod's natural landscapes. The trail meanders through pine forests, cranberry bogs, and salt marshes, offering a glimpse into the region's diverse ecosystems. Along the way, cyclists and walkers can enjoy sightings of various bird species, including ospreys, herons, and shorebirds, as well as other wildlife such as deer and turtles.

Outdoor Recreation:

CAPE COD RAIL TRAIL

The Cape Cod Rail Trail provides ample opportunities for outdoor recreation and leisure activities. Cycling is one of the most popular activities on the trail, with its smooth pavement and gentle slopes catering to riders of all ages and skill levels. Rental shops can be found near the trail, allowing visitors to easily obtain bicycles for their Cape Cod adventure.

In addition to cycling, the trail welcomes walkers, joggers, and inline skaters. The wide, well-maintained path ensures a comfortable and enjoyable experience for all users. Picnic areas and rest stops are scattered along the trail, providing places to rest, refuel, and take in the surroundings.

Exploring Cape Cod Towns:

One of the unique aspects of the Cape Cod Rail Trail is its proximity to several charming Cape Cod towns. Riders and walkers can take detours along the trail to explore the shops, galleries, restaurants, and historic sites of towns such as Orleans, Brewster, and Wellfleet. These towns offer a glimpse into Cape Cod's rich cultural heritage, and visitors can sample local cuisine, browse through unique boutiques, or visit museums and art galleries.

Community Engagement and Events:

The Cape Cod Rail Trail is not just a recreational pathway; it is also a symbol of community engagement and a hub for events and activities. Local organizations and community groups often organize events along the trail, fostering a sense of camaraderie and encouraging people to come together and enjoy the outdoors.

Throughout the year, various events take place along the Cape Cod Rail Trail, catering to different interests and age groups. These events may include charity walks, bike rides, nature walks, art exhibits, and cultural festivals. Participating in these events not only allows visitors to engage with the local community but also provides an opportunity to support local causes and initiatives.

Accessibility and Amenities:

The Cape Cod Rail Trail is designed to be accessible to people of all abilities. The trail features wheelchair-friendly sections and is equipped with amenities such as restrooms, water stations, and informational signage. Additionally, several parking areas are available along the trail, making it convenient for visitors to access different sections of the pathway.

Environmental Stewardship:

The Cape Cod Rail Trail is committed to environmental stewardship and sustainable practices. Efforts are made to preserve the natural habitats, protect wildlife, and promote responsible trail use. Visitors are encouraged to follow trail etiquette, respect wildlife and vegetation, and dispose of waste properly.

Future Expansion:

The popularity of the Cape Cod Rail Trail has led to discussions and plans for its expansion. Proposed extensions aim to connect the existing trail to additional towns and attractions, further enhancing the trail's accessibility and allowing visitors to explore more of Cape Cod's beauty.

10

Chatham Lighthouse

The Chatham Lighthouse, perched on the southeastern tip of Cape Cod in Massachusetts, is a beacon of maritime history and a symbol of the town of Chatham. With its rich history, picturesque setting, and vital role in guiding ships safely through treacherous waters, the Chatham Lighthouse has become an iconic landmark and a must-visit destination for locals and visitors alike.

The Chatham Lighthouse has a storied history that dates back to the early 19th century. The first lighthouse on the site was constructed in 1808 to aid ships navigating the dangerous waters off Chatham's coastline. However, due to erosion and deterioration, it was replaced by a new lighthouse in 1841. This second lighthouse, which still stands today, was built using locally sourced bricks and featured a distinctive Cape Cod-style architecture.

The Chatham Lighthouse has played a crucial role in guiding ships through the Chatham Bar, a treacherous sandbar that poses a significant hazard to maritime navigation. Its powerful light and fog signal have helped mariners safely navigate these challenging waters, reducing the risk of shipwrecks and saving countless lives throughout its history.

Architecture and Design:

The Chatham Lighthouse exhibits the classic Cape Cod-style architecture that is characteristic of the region. The tower stands at a height of 48 feet and is painted in alternating white and black bands, a distinctive feature that aids in its identification during daylight hours. The lantern room atop the tower houses a powerful rotating beacon that emits a bright light visible for miles out to sea.

Adjacent to the lighthouse tower is the keeper's house, a charming two-story building that once served as the residence for the lighthouse keepers and their families. The keeper's house has been well-preserved and now houses the Chatham Lighthouse Museum, where visitors can learn about the history and significance of the lighthouse through exhibits, artifacts, and historical photographs.

Lighthouse Beach:

The Chatham Lighthouse is located in close proximity to Lighthouse Beach, a stunning stretch of coastline that draws visitors with its pristine sandy shores and panoramic views. The beach offers a tranquil setting for sunbathing, picnicking, and leisurely walks along the shoreline. From the beach, visitors can enjoy breathtaking vistas of the lighthouse against the backdrop of the Atlantic Ocean, creating a postcard-worthy scene that captures the essence of Cape Cod's coastal charm.

Observing the Lighthouse:

While visitors are not allowed to enter the lighthouse tower itself, they can still appreciate its beauty and significance from the surrounding areas. The Chatham Lighthouse is visible from various vantage points, allowing visitors to capture stunning photographs and admire its architecture and maritime heritage.

One of the best spots to view the lighthouse is from Chatham Light Beach, located on the opposite side of the lighthouse. This beach offers a different perspective, allowing visitors to see the tower from a unique angle and appreciate its striking presence against the coastal landscape.

Visiting the Chatham Lighthouse Museum:

A visit to the Chatham Lighthouse would not be complete without exploring the Chatham Lighthouse Museum. Housed in the keeper's house, the museum offers a captivating glimpse into the history of the lighthouse and its role in maritime navigation. Exhibits showcase artifacts, historical documents, and interactive displays, providing visitors with a deeper understanding of the lighthouse's significance and its impact on the local community.

Special Events and Tours:

Throughout the year, the Chatham Lighthouse hosts special events and tours that allow visitors to further immerse themselves in its rich history.

These events may include guided tours of the lighthouse and keeper's house, where visitors can climb the steps of the tower and enjoy panoramic views from the lantern room. These tours provide a unique opportunity to learn about the inner workings of the lighthouse and the daily life of the keepers who tended to it.

In addition to tours, the Chatham Lighthouse often hosts community events and celebrations. One notable event is the annual Chatham Lighthouse Lighting, held during the holiday season. This festive event brings the community together to witness the illumination of the lighthouse with a stunning display of lights, creating a magical atmosphere and spreading holiday cheer.

Maritime Heritage and Coastal Preservation:
   The Chatham Lighthouse serves as a reminder of Cape Cod's rich maritime heritage and the vital role lighthouses played in guiding ships along its coastline. It stands as a testament to the bravery and dedication of the keepers who tended to the light, ensuring the safety of mariners and the preservation of coastal communities.

The lighthouse also serves as a symbol of the importance of coastal preservation. Its location near the Chatham Bar highlights the need for environmental stewardship and the protection of delicate coastal ecosystems. The town of Chatham, in collaboration with various organizations, works diligently to preserve the natural beauty of the area and maintain the integrity of the lighthouse and its surroundings.

Scenic Beauty and Outdoor Activities:
   Beyond its historical and cultural significance, the Chatham Lighthouse offers visitors the opportunity to engage in a variety of outdoor activities. Lighthouse Beach, with its pristine sands

and stunning vistas, invites beachgoers to relax, swim, and enjoy the beauty of the Atlantic Ocean. The beach is also a popular spot for surfers, who ride the waves generated by the nearby Chatham Bar.

For nature enthusiasts, the Chatham Lighthouse area provides ample opportunities for birdwatching, as numerous bird species frequent the coastal habitats. Visitors may spot ospreys, shorebirds, and even the occasional seal basking in the sun on nearby sandbars.

11

Sandwich Village

Sandwich Village, located on Cape Cod in Massachusetts, is a picturesque and historic destination that showcases the charm and character of a quintessential New England town. As the oldest town on Cape Cod, Sandwich holds a rich history that is reflected in its well-preserved architecture, quaint streets, and cultural attractions.

Sandwich Village was settled in 1637 and holds the distinction of being the oldest town on Cape Cod. Its historical significance is evident in the beautifully preserved homes and buildings that line the streets, many of which date back to the 18th and 19th centuries. Walking through the village, visitors can immerse themselves in the town's colonial past, admiring the architectural styles that have stood the test of time.

Heritage Museums and Gardens:
One of the premier attractions in Sandwich Village is the Heritage Museums and Gardens, a cultural and natural history complex that offers a unique blend of art, gardens, and exhibits.

The museum showcases a diverse collection of Americana, including folk art, antique automobiles, and a renowned collection of American firearms. Visitors can explore the art galleries, stroll through meticulously manicured gardens, and even take a ride on a vintage carousel. The Heritage Museums and Gardens provide a comprehensive experience that appeals to visitors of all ages.

Sandwich Glass Museum:

Sandwich Village is also famous for its glassmaking history, and the Sandwich Glass Museum pays homage to this important industry. The museum displays a remarkable collection of glassware, including stunning examples of Sandwich glass, which was produced in the town from the early 19th century until the late 1880s. Visitors can witness live glassblowing demonstrations, learn about the techniques used in the production of Sandwich glass, and explore the fascinating history of this once-thriving industry.

Historic Attractions:

Sandwich Village boasts a wealth of historic attractions that transport visitors back in time. The Dexter Grist Mill, built in 1637, is one such attraction and is considered the oldest mill on Cape Cod. Visitors can see the fully operational mill grinding cornmeal and learn about its role in the town's early development.

The Hoxie House, built around 1675, is another notable historic site in Sandwich Village. This saltbox-style house is one of the oldest surviving houses in Massachusetts and provides a glimpse into the lives of the early settlers. Guided tours offer insight into the daily routines and challenges faced by the original inhabitants.

Quaint Streets and Unique Shops:

The streets of Sandwich Village are lined with charming boutiques, galleries, and specialty shops, making it a delightful destination for shoppers. Visitors can explore a wide range of offerings, including local artisan crafts, antiques, and Cape Cod-inspired gifts. The Village Green, a picturesque park in the center of town, provides a tranquil setting for a leisurely stroll or a picnic lunch.

Outdoor Recreation:

Sandwich Village is also a haven for outdoor enthusiasts. The town is bordered by scenic waterways, including the Cape Cod Canal and Shawme Pond, offering opportunities for boating, fishing, and kayaking. Shawme-Crowell State Forest, located just outside the village, features hiking trails that wind through serene woodlands, providing a peaceful escape into nature.

Cultural Events and Festivals:

Throughout the year, Sandwich Village comes alive with cultural events and festivals that celebrate its heritage and local talent. The Heritage Museums and Gardens host outdoor concerts, art exhibits, and craft fairs, providing a vibrant cultural scene. The Sandwich Artisans Outdoor Market, held on the Village Green, showcases the work of local artists.

Sandwich Village boasts a wealth of historic attractions that transport visitors back in time. The Dexter Grist Mill, built in 1637, is one such attraction and is considered the oldest mill on Cape Cod. Visitors can see the fully operational mill grinding cornmeal and learn about its role in the town's early development.

Outdoor Recreation:

Sandwich Village is also a haven for outdoor enthusiasts. The town is bordered by scenic waterways, including the Cape Cod Canal and Shawme Pond, offering opportunities for boating, fishing, and kayaking. Shawme-Crowell State Forest, located just outside the village, features hiking trails that wind through serene woodlands, providing a peaceful escape into nature.

Historic Sandwich Village Inn:

For visitors seeking a truly immersive experience in the heart of Sandwich Village, the Historic Sandwich Village Inn provides a charming and comfortable accommodation option. Located in a beautifully restored 1805 building, the inn offers cozy rooms, modern amenities, and warm hospitality. Guests can enjoy a delicious breakfast in the morning and explore the village's attractions and dining options just steps away.

Annual Sandwich Festivals:

Sandwich Village is renowned for its lively and festive events, drawing crowds from near and far. The Sandwich Glass Town Cultural District hosts the Annual Glassblowers' Christmas, where visitors can witness glass artists creating stunning holiday-themed pieces. The Sandwich Town Fair is another popular event, featuring carnival rides, live entertainment, local food vendors, and agricultural exhibits. These annual festivals bring the community together and provide a fun-filled experience for all ages.

IV

Historic Sites and Museums

We will now learn in more detail about these historical sites, a lot of which we have learned about a little about in the previous part of this book.

12

Plimoth Plantation

Nestled on the picturesque shores of Cape Cod, Massachusetts, Plimoth Plantation stands as a living testament to the early English settlement of America. This historical site and museum offer visitors a captivating glimpse into the lives of the Pilgrims and Native Americans who played a significant role in shaping the foundation of the United States. Embark on a remarkable journey back in time as we delve into the rich history and immersive experiences that await at Plimoth Plantation.

Plimoth Plantation, founded in 1947, aims to recreate the original settlement of Plymouth Colony, established by the Pilgrims in 1620. Stepping foot into the plantation is like stepping into the past. Authenticity permeates every corner, from the meticulously reconstructed buildings to the period clothing worn by interpreters who bring history to life. The plantation offers a unique opportunity to witness firsthand the challenges and triumphs of the Pilgrims' early colonial life.

One of the main highlights of Plimoth Plantation is the 17th-century English Village, a painstaking replica of the original settlement. Stroll along dirt paths and interact with costumed interpreters who skillfully portray actual Pilgrim residents. Engage in conversations about their daily routines, farming techniques, and religious beliefs. Immerse yourself in the day-to-day activities of the villagers as they weave textiles, cook over an open hearth, and tend to their livestock. The village is a living history lesson, allowing visitors to gain a profound understanding of the Pilgrims' struggles and resilience.

Beyond the English Village, Plimoth Plantation extends its focus to the Native Americans who encountered the Pilgrims upon their arrival. The Wampanoag Homesite presents a faithful reproduction of a 17th-century Native American settlement, providing an invaluable glimpse into the culture and traditions of the indigenous people. Engage in conversations with Native interpreters, who share their ancestral knowledge, demonstrate traditional crafts, and provide insight into their way of life. Gain a deep appreciation for the complex relationship between the Pilgrims and the Native Americans, discovering the challenges they faced as they navigated their differences and sought to coexist.

The educational experiences at Plimoth Plantation extend beyond the villages themselves. The Craft Center showcases traditional crafts such as blacksmithing, pottery, and woodworking, allowing visitors to witness the artisans' skill and dedication firsthand. Interactive exhibits and workshops offer the opportunity to try one's hand at these crafts, fostering a deeper appreciation for the craftsmanship of the period.

For a more comprehensive understanding of the history and significance of Plimoth Plantation, a visit to the Mayflower II is a must. This full-scale reproduction of the original Mayflower ship provides a glimpse into the challenging transatlantic journey undertaken by the Pilgrims. Step aboard and explore the cramped quarters, witness the difficult conditions faced by the passengers, and gain a profound appreciation for their courage and determination.

Plimoth Plantation goes beyond its physical exhibits by offering a variety of educational programs and events. From immersive school field trips to historical reenactments and themed celebrations, there are numerous opportunities for visitors of all ages to engage with history in a hands-on and dynamic way.

13

Heritage Museums & Gardens

Nestled in the heart of Cape Cod, Massachusetts, Heritage Museums & Gardens is a treasure trove of natural beauty, rich history, and captivating exhibits. Spanning over 100 acres, this expansive museum and garden complex offers visitors a unique and immersive experience, combining stunning landscapes, engaging exhibitions, and a deep appreciation for the region's heritage. Join us as we embark on a journey through the diverse attractions and breathtaking scenery that make Heritage Museums & Gardens a must-visit destination.

Heritage Museums & Gardens seamlessly blends nature and culture, showcasing a diverse range of gardens, art installations, and historical exhibits. One of the highlights of the complex is the extensive collection of gardens, meticulously designed to provide a sensory feast for visitors. From the rhododendron-laden Flume Garden to the serene tranquility of the Japanese Garden, each area offers a unique ambiance and a vibrant display of color and fragrance. Stroll along winding paths, breathe in the floral scents, and immerse yourself in the serene beauty of nature.

The museum's horticultural wonders are complemented by a stunning collection of American folk art and antique automobiles. The American Art & Carousel Gallery houses an impressive assemblage of folk art, including intricate carvings, weathervanes, and decorative arts that showcase the creativity and craftsmanship of American artists. Additionally, the Automobile Gallery features a remarkable collection of antique cars, providing a glimpse into the evolution of automotive design and engineering throughout the decades. Marvel at the elegance of vintage automobiles and appreciate their historical significance within the broader context of American culture.

For history enthusiasts, the Heritage Museum Building offers a captivating journey into the region's past. Explore the Cape Cod History Exhibits, which chronicle the area's maritime heritage, the development of local industries, and the lives of early settlers. Engage with interactive displays, examine historical artifacts, and gain a deeper understanding of Cape Cod's unique cultural identity. The exhibits provide a comprehensive overview of the region's history, from its Native American roots to its role in shaping the maritime trade routes of the Atlantic.

Another standout feature of Heritage Museums & Gardens is the Hidden Hollow, an interactive outdoor learning area designed for children and families. This enchanting space encourages young visitors to connect with nature and engage in imaginative play. Kids can explore the woodland setting, climb treehouses, build forts, and embark on nature-inspired adventures. The

Hidden Hollow fosters a love for the outdoors and a sense of wonder, offering a space where children can learn and play in harmony with nature.

In addition to its permanent exhibits, Heritage Museums & Gardens hosts a variety of special events and temporary exhibitions throughout the year. From art shows and garden festivals to horticultural workshops and live performances, there is always something exciting happening on the museum grounds. These events provide an opportunity to engage with artists, horticulturists, and historians, further enriching the visitor experience and fostering a sense of community.

To complete the Heritage Museums & Gardens experience, a visit to the Hidden Hollow Café is a must. Indulge in a delectable selection of locally sourced and seasonal fare while enjoying panoramic views of the gardens. The café provides a delightful culinary experience, allowing visitors to relax and rejuvenate amidst the natural splendor that surrounds them.

14

Cape Cod Museum of Art

The Cape Cod Museum of Art, located in Dennis, Massachusetts, is a cultural gem on the Cape that showcases a rich collection of American art, specifically highlighting the unique artistic expression of Cape Cod and its surrounding regions. The museum's mission is to celebrate the rich artistic heritage of the region and inspire creativity and engagement with the arts.

The museum is housed in a beautifully restored 19th-century building, which was once a Cape Cod sea captain's home. The interior of the museum is elegant and welcoming, with an intimate feel that encourages visitors to linger and explore. The Cape Cod Museum of Art houses a collection of over 2,000 works of art, including paintings, sculptures, and photographs, with a strong focus on contemporary and modern art from the region.

One of the highlights of the museum's collection is its extensive holdings of works by the Cape Cod School of Art, a group of artists who flourished on the Cape in the early 20th century.

The Cape Cod School of Art was founded by renowned artists such as Charles W. Hawthorne and Frank W. Benson, who were drawn to the natural beauty of the region and inspired by its unique light and landscape. The museum's collection includes works by many of the leading figures of the Cape Cod School of Art, providing a fascinating glimpse into the artistic movements of the time and the region's cultural heritage.

In addition to its permanent collection, the Cape Cod Museum of Art hosts a dynamic range of exhibitions throughout the year, showcasing a diverse range of artists and styles. From solo shows by emerging artists to group exhibitions exploring specific themes or media, the museum's exhibitions are always fresh, engaging, and thought-provoking. The museum also hosts a range of educational programs, including lectures, workshops, and tours, aimed at fostering greater appreciation and understanding of the arts.

One of the unique aspects of the Cape Cod Museum of Art is its commitment to showcasing the work of local artists, providing a platform for emerging and established artists from the region to exhibit their work. The museum's Community Gallery is dedicated to showcasing the work of local artists, providing a space for them to display their work and connect with the community. The museum also hosts an annual Cape Cod Art Center Juried Exhibition, which showcases the work of artists from across the region, celebrating the diversity and vibrancy of the local arts scene.

Beyond its exhibitions and educational programs, the Cape Cod Museum of Art offers visitors a range of opportunities to engage with the arts. The museum's ArtCafé offers a range of delicious and locally sourced food and drink, with indoor and outdoor seating options overlooking the beautiful grounds. The museum's ArtWorks gift shop offers a range of unique gifts, jewelry, and home decor, featuring the work of local artists and artisans. The museum also hosts a range of social events throughout the year, providing a space for visitors to connect with the arts and each other.

The Cape Cod Museum of Art is also known for its stunning sculpture garden, which features works by local and regional artists set amongst the beautiful landscape. The sculpture garden is a peaceful and contemplative space, providing visitors with an opportunity to engage with art in an outdoor setting. The museum's grounds are also home to the beautiful Little Creek Nature Area, which features walking trails, a salt marsh, and a pond, offering visitors a chance to explore the natural beauty of Cape Cod.

15

Edward Gorey House

Tucked away in the quaint town of Yarmouth Port, Massachusetts, the Edward Gorey House stands as a whimsical and eccentric museum dedicated to the life and work of the enigmatic artist and writer, Edward Gorey. Known for his dark and humorous illustrations, Gorey captivated audiences with his distinctive style and macabre sensibility. This unique museum invites visitors to step into the world of Gorey, exploring his art, literature, and quirky personality. Join us on a journey through the fascinating and delightfully peculiar Edward Gorey House.

The Edward Gorey House is located in the very home where the artist himself lived from 1986 until his passing in 2000. The museum is a testament to Gorey's whimsical and eccentric spirit, providing visitors with an intimate and immersive experience. As you approach the house, you'll immediately notice the distinctive black exterior, adorned with ironwork and adorned gables, giving it an air of mystery and intrigue.

Upon entering the museum, visitors are transported into the captivating universe of Edward Gorey. The rooms are carefully curated to reflect Gorey's unique aesthetic, filled with memorabilia, artifacts, and original artwork. The house is an artistic labyrinth, inviting guests to explore the different facets of Gorey's life and creativity.

One of the highlights of the Edward Gorey House is the exhibition of Gorey's original artwork, including his pen and ink drawings, book illustrations, and set designs. The artwork showcases Gorey's distinct style, characterized by his intricate cross-hatching, Victorian-inspired characters, and his playful yet macabre narratives. The exhibition provides a comprehensive overview of Gorey's artistic career, spanning his early works to his collaborations with renowned authors and his own published books.

Beyond the artwork, the museum delves into the fascinating aspects of Gorey's life and influences. Visitors can explore his vast collection of objects, such as antique toys, found objects, and curiosities that he amassed throughout his lifetime. These artifacts offer insights into Gorey's unique sensibilities and his penchant for the odd and unconventional. Additionally, the museum features personal items and mementos, giving visitors a glimpse into Gorey's private world and his multifaceted personality.

One of the most charming aspects of the Edward Gorey House is the attention to detail and whimsical touches throughout the museum. From the eclectic furnishings to the cat-shaped weathervane on the roof, every corner reflects Gorey's idiosyncratic taste and offbeat sense of humor. Visitors can enjoy interactive elements, including a scavenger hunt, where they can search for hidden objects and references in Gorey's artwork.

The museum also offers a range of programs and events that celebrate Gorey's art and literature. These include readings of his works, lectures on his life and career, and workshops inspired by his creative process. These events provide opportunities for visitors to engage with Gorey's work on a deeper level and to appreciate the lasting impact he has had on the art world.

The Edward Gorey House gift shop is a must-visit for fans of the artist. It offers a wide selection of Gorey-inspired merchandise, including books, prints, clothing, and housewares. Visitors can take a piece of Gorey's whimsy home with them, allowing his unique artistic vision to continue to inspire and enchant.

16

Whydah Pirate Museum

Located in the historic town of Provincetown, Massachusetts, the Whydah Pirate Museum stands as a captivating testament to the Golden Age of Piracy. This unique museum takes visitors on an immersive journey through history, unveiling the story of the Whydah, a notorious pirate ship that met a dramatic end off the coast of Cape Cod. Prepare to embark on an extraordinary adventure as we explore the treasures and tales within the Whydah Pirate Museum.

The Whydah Pirate Museum is dedicated to preserving the legacy of the Whydah Gally, a fully rigged 18th-century pirate ship captained by the infamous pirate Samuel "Black Sam" Bellamy. The ship, originally a slaving vessel, was captured by Bellamy in 1717 and transformed into one of the most feared pirate ships of its time. The Whydah was known for its audacious attacks on merchant vessels and its vast treasure hoard.

At the heart of the museum is a remarkable collection of artifacts recovered from the wreckage of the Whydah. These relics provide a tangible connection to the ship and its crew, offering a unique glimpse into the world of pirates. Visitors can marvel at the treasure chests, cannons, weapons, and personal items recovered from the shipwreck, all of which are displayed in meticulous detail.

One of the highlights of the museum is the interactive exhibits that bring the story of the Whydah to life. Visitors can step into a replica of the Whydah's captain's cabin, experiencing the living quarters of a pirate captain firsthand. They can also learn about the daily lives of the crew, their roles aboard the ship, and the challenges they faced on the high seas. Through multimedia presentations and immersive displays, the museum captures the spirit of the pirate era and engages visitors in an educational and entertaining way.

The Whydah Pirate Museum also offers insights into the archaeological excavation and recovery process that led to the discovery of the shipwreck. The story of the Whydah's discovery and the ongoing efforts to preserve and study its artifacts are showcased, providing visitors with a behind-the-scenes look at the work of underwater archaeologists. The museum's commitment to historical accuracy and meticulous research ensures that the exhibits offer a comprehensive and accurate portrayal of the ship and its history.

In addition to the permanent exhibits, the Whydah Pirate Museum hosts a range of educational programs and events. These include guided tours, lectures, and hands-on activities that cater to visitors of all ages. The museum provides a wealth of information about pirate history, maritime archaeology, and the cultural significance of the Golden Age of Piracy. These programs allow visitors to delve deeper into the fascinating world of pirates and gain a greater understanding of their impact on maritime history.

For those seeking a tangible connection to the pirate era, the museum offers the opportunity to touch real pirate treasure. Visitors can hold authentic coins and other artifacts recovered from the Whydah wreck, allowing them to experience the thrill of discovering buried treasure firsthand.

The Whydah Pirate Museum gift shop offers a wide range of pirate-themed merchandise, including books, clothing, and souvenirs. Visitors can take home a piece of pirate history, allowing the adventure to continue beyond the museum walls.

V

Outdoor Dining and Local Cuisine

17

Fresh Seafood and Lobster Shacks

When it comes to outdoor dining on Cape Cod, few things evoke the essence of the region more than fresh seafood and lobster shacks. With its proximity to the Atlantic Ocean and rich maritime heritage, Cape Cod is renowned for its bountiful seafood offerings, including succulent lobster, mouthwatering clams, and delectable fish. Join us as we embark on a culinary journey through the vibrant world of fresh seafood and lobster shacks, where you can savor the flavors of the sea in a relaxed and picturesque outdoor setting.

Cape Cod is dotted with a myriad of seafood shacks, each offering its unique twist on fresh seafood cuisine. These shacks are often located along the coastline, allowing diners to enjoy the gentle sea breeze and breathtaking ocean views while indulging in their favorite seafood delicacies.

Lobster shacks, in particular, are a quintessential part of the Cape Cod dining experience. These humble establishments serve up some of the most mouthwatering lobster dishes you'll ever taste. From classic lobster rolls, where tender chunks of lobster meat are nestled in a buttered, toasted bun, to whole lobsters steamed to perfection, lobster shacks are a haven for seafood lovers. Picture yourself sitting at a picnic table, cracking open a freshly cooked lobster and savoring every juicy bite, all while soaking in the coastal ambiance.

One beloved lobster shack on Cape Cod is the iconic Arnold's Lobster & Clam Bar in Eastham. Established in 1976, this family-owned institution has been delighting locals and visitors alike with its exceptional seafood offerings. In addition to their renowned lobster rolls, Arnold's serves up an array of seafood favorites, including fried clams, scallops, and fish and chips. The outdoor seating area is spacious and relaxed, with colorful picnic tables nestled amongst the sand dunes, providing a perfect setting to enjoy your meal.

Another must-visit spot is the Sesuit Harbor Cafe in Dennis. This picturesque waterfront eatery offers stunning views of the harbor and serves up some of the freshest seafood on Cape Cod. Indulge in their famous lobster rolls or opt for other seafood delights such as oysters, clams, and shrimp. With its casual atmosphere and waterfront location, the Sesuit Harbor Cafe is an ideal spot to soak in the coastal charm while savoring the flavors of the sea.

For those seeking a more casual and off-the-beaten-path experience, the Beachcomber in Wellfleet is a hidden gem. Located right on the beach, this laid-back seafood shack offers a relaxed atmosphere and panoramic ocean views. Feast on their renowned clam chowder, crispy fish tacos, or their signature lobster bisque, all while enjoying live music and the refreshing sea breeze. The Beachcomber embodies the essence of Cape Cod's beach culture, making it a must-visit destination for seafood enthusiasts and beach lovers alike.

In addition to lobster shacks, Cape Cod boasts a wide variety of seafood restaurants and fish markets where you can indulge in an array of fresh catches. Whether you're in the mood for local oysters, succulent scallops, or flaky cod, these establishments are dedicated to providing the highest quality seafood straight from the ocean to your plate.

One such notable seafood restaurant is the Chatham Pier Fish Market in Chatham. Located right on the fish pier, this establishment offers a unique dining experience where you can watch the fishing boats come in with their daily catch. Sample their famous fish and chips, try their lobster bisque, or opt for a plate of freshly shucked oysters. With its waterfront location and charming atmosphere, the Chatham Pier Fish Market is a favorite among seafood connoisseurs.

For those looking to take the culinary adventure beyond lobster shacks, the Cape Cod region is home to numerous seafood restaurants that offer outdoor dining experiences. One such establishment is The Lobster Pot in Provincetown, which has been serving up fresh seafood since 1979. Known for its extensive menu and waterfront location, The Lobster Pot offers panoramic views of Provincetown Harbor, creating a picturesque backdrop for enjoying their delicious seafood dishes. From their famous clam chowder and lobster bisque to their baked stuffed lobster and seafood paella, this restaurant presents a wide range of seafood options that cater to every palate.

Another notable seafood dining destination is the Wicked Oyster in Wellfleet. Situated in the heart of the town, this charming eatery offers an inviting outdoor patio where you can enjoy their delectable seafood offerings. Indulge in their raw bar featuring locally sourced oysters, clams, and shrimp, or opt for their seafood specialties such as pan-seared scallops, grilled swordfish, or stuffed sole. With its emphasis on fresh and locally sourced ingredients, the Wicked Oyster provides a true taste of Cape Cod's culinary heritage.

When it comes to outdoor seafood dining, Cape Cod truly offers an abundance of options. Whether you prefer the rustic charm of a lobster shack or the refined ambiance of a waterfront restaurant, there's something for everyone to enjoy. From the simplicity of a perfectly prepared lobster roll to the complexity of a seafood feast, each dish tells a story of Cape Cod's rich maritime heritage and culinary traditions.

As you embark on your culinary journey through Cape Cod, be sure to savor the flavors of the sea, embrace the coastal charm, and indulge in the freshest seafood that the region has to offer. Whether you're a seafood enthusiast or simply appreciate a good meal in a picturesque setting, the outdoor dining experiences found in fresh seafood and lobster shacks will leave you with unforgettable memories and a true taste of Cape Cod's culinary delights.

18

Farm-to-Table Restaurants

In recent years, the farm-to-table movement has gained significant momentum, emphasizing the importance of fresh, locally sourced ingredients in culinary experiences. Nowhere is this philosophy more evident than in the thriving farm-to-table restaurant scene on Cape Cod. These establishments embrace the concept of sustainability, supporting local farmers and artisans while offering diners a unique and memorable culinary journey. Join us as we delve into the world of farm-to-table restaurants on Cape Cod and discover the delights of dining on locally grown, seasonal fare.

At the heart of the farm-to-table movement is the desire to connect consumers with the source of their food and promote a sustainable food system. Cape Cod's fertile lands and coastal proximity make it an ideal location for farm-to-table restaurants to thrive. These establishments prioritize working closely with local farmers, fishermen, and purveyors to create menus that highlight the region's seasonal bounty.

One exemplary farm-to-table restaurant on Cape Cod is The Canteen in Provincetown. This charming eatery is dedicated to showcasing the best of Cape Cod's local produce, seafood, and artisanal products. The Canteen sources ingredients directly from nearby farms and fishermen, ensuring that each dish reflects the flavors of the region. Diners can enjoy creative and seasonal dishes such as beet and goat cheese salad, locally caught fish tacos, and farm-fresh vegetable bowls. The menu changes regularly to showcase the freshest ingredients available, offering a culinary adventure that celebrates the essence of farm-to-table dining.

Another standout farm-to-table destination is PB Boulangerie Bistro in Wellfleet. This French-inspired bistro not only serves up exquisite baked goods but also embraces the farm-to-table ethos. The restaurant partners with local farmers, foragers, and fishermen to curate a menu that highlights the best of Cape Cod's agricultural and maritime offerings. From their farm-fresh salads to their seafood bouillabaisse and grass-fed beef dishes, PB Boulangerie Bistro crafts dishes that are a true reflection of the region's seasonal abundance. With its warm and inviting atmosphere, this restaurant provides a memorable farm-to-table dining experience that is both comforting and indulgent.

One unique farm-to-table gem is the Blackfish restaurant in Truro. Nestled in an old farmhouse, Blackfish offers a rustic and intimate setting where guests can savor the flavors of Cape Cod's local ingredients. The restaurant's commitment to sustainable practices is evident in their menu, which features dishes made with locally raised meats, organic vegetables, and fresh seafood. Whether it's their roasted Atlantic halibut, cider-braised pork shoulder, or seasonal vegetable medley, each dish is a celebration of the region's agricultural richness. Blackfish also collaborates with local farmers and artisans, hosting special events and themed dinners that showcase the diversity and quality of Cape Cod's culinary community.

Beyond their delectable menus, farm-to-table restaurants on Cape Cod often boast charming settings that further enhance the dining experience. Many establishments are housed in historic buildings or scenic locations, offering picturesque views and a connection to the region's cultural heritage. Whether it's dining in a restored farmhouse, overlooking a vineyard, or enjoying a meal in a garden setting, the ambiance of these restaurants adds an extra layer of enjoyment to the farm-to-table experience.

In addition to supporting local farmers and purveyors, farm-to-table restaurants often prioritize sustainable practices, such as composting, recycling, and minimizing food waste. By focusing on sustainable sourcing and reducing their carbon footprint, these establishments contribute to the preservation of Cape Cod's natural beauty and resources, ensuring that future generations can continue to enjoy the region's agricultural and culinary heritage.

The farm-to-table movement on Cape Cod not only celebrates the flavors of the land
    and sea but also fosters a sense of community. Many farm-to-table restaurants actively engage with their local communities by hosting farm tours, collaborating with nearby schools, and participating in farmers' markets and food festivals. These

initiatives not only educate diners about the importance of sustainable food practices but also strengthen the bonds between farmers, chefs, and consumers.

One such example is the Cape Cod Organic Farm in Barnstable. This working farm not only supplies fresh, organic produce to local farm-to-table restaurants but also opens its doors to the community. Visitors can take guided tours of the farm, participate in workshops, and even lend a hand in the fields. The farm's on-site café serves up delicious meals made with ingredients straight from the fields, providing visitors with a true farm-to-table experience. The Cape Cod Organic Farm exemplifies the farm-to-table ethos by fostering a deep connection between the land, the community, and the dining table.

Farm-to-table restaurants also play a vital role in promoting culinary creativity and innovation. Chefs who embrace the farm-to-table philosophy are constantly challenged to craft menus that reflect the seasonal availability of ingredients. This dynamic approach to cooking encourages chefs to experiment with flavors, textures, and techniques, resulting in dishes that are both inspired and ever-changing. As a result, dining at a farm-to-table restaurant is not just a meal but an opportunity to embark on a culinary adventure, where each visit brings the excitement of discovering new flavors and combinations.

Moreover, farm-to-table dining on Cape Cod offers a chance to experience the unique terroir of the region. The combination of fertile soil, salt air, and ocean breezes lends a distinct character to the local produce and seafood. From the briny oysters of Wellfleet to the tender greens of Truro, each ingredient carries the essence of Cape Cod's coastal landscape. By showcasing these flavors, farm-to-table restaurants create a deeper connection to the region's culinary heritage and invite diners to savor the essence of Cape Cod on every plate.

19

Local Breweries and Wineries

When it comes to craft beverages, Cape Cod offers a flourishing scene of local breweries and wineries that tantalize the taste buds of residents and visitors alike. Nestled amidst the scenic landscapes and coastal beauty, these establishments showcase the region's commitment to quality and innovation. Join us on a journey through the world of local breweries and wineries on Cape Cod as we discover the liquid delights that make this region a haven for craft beverage enthusiasts.

Cape Cod's craft beer scene has experienced remarkable growth in recent years, with a plethora of breweries crafting unique and flavorful brews. These local breweries are dedicated to using high-quality ingredients, experimenting with innovative recipes, and creating a welcoming atmosphere for patrons to enjoy their libations.

One standout brewery on Cape Cod is Cape Cod Beer in Hyannis. Founded in 2004, this family-owned and operated brewery has become a beloved staple in the local community. Cape Cod Beer prides itself on using locally sourced ingredients whenever possible, including Cape Cod cranberries and honey. Their lineup of beers reflects the region's character, featuring refreshing brews like Cape Cod Blonde, Beach Blonde Ale, and Cape Cod IPA. Visitors can take a tour of the brewery, witness the brewing process, and sample a variety of beers in the welcoming taproom. With its commitment to quality and community engagement, Cape Cod Beer embodies the spirit of local craft brewing.

Another notable brewery is Devil's Purse Brewing Company in South Dennis. Inspired by the traditional brewing methods of European farmhouse ales, Devil's Purse combines Old World brewing techniques with local ingredients to create unique and distinctive beers. From their German-style Kolsch to their Belgian-inspired saisons and barrel-aged creations, Devil's Purse offers a diverse range of flavors that captivate the palate. The brewery's taproom provides a cozy and relaxed atmosphere where visitors can savor their brews while engaging with the passionate team behind the operation.

In addition to breweries, Cape Cod boasts several wineries that produce exceptional wines, showcasing the region's ability to cultivate grapes and craft elegant vintages. These wineries take advantage of the coastal climate, producing wines that reflect the terroir of Cape Cod.

Truro Vineyards of Cape Cod is a renowned winery that has been captivating wine enthusiasts since 1991. Set on 11 acres of beautiful land, the vineyard cultivates various grape varietals, including Chardonnay, Cabernet Franc, and Merlot. Truro Vineyards offers guided tours, allowing visitors to explore the vineyard and learn about the winemaking process. The winery's tasting room invites guests to sample their award-winning wines, such as their crisp white blends, rich reds, and delightful rosés. With its stunning surroundings and dedication to producing exceptional wines, Truro Vineyards is a must-visit destination for wine lovers.

Another gem in the Cape Cod wine scene is First Crush Winery in Harwich. This boutique winery focuses on small-batch production and handcrafted wines, using grapes sourced from their own vineyard and select vineyards throughout Massachusetts. First Crush Winery's commitment to quality and attention to detail is evident in every bottle they produce. From their aromatic white wines to their full-bodied reds, each wine tells a story of Cape Cod's unique winemaking journey. Visitors can enjoy tastings in the intimate tasting room, where they can engage with the passionate winemakers and gain insights into the winemaking process.

What sets Cape Cod's local breweries and wineries apart is their sense of community and connection to the region. Many of these establishments actively participate in local events, support local causes, and collaborate with nearby businesses. They often serve as gathering spaces for friends, families and neighbors to come together and celebrate the region's liquid creations. From hosting live music events to organizing beer and wine festivals, these establishments contribute to the vibrant cultural fabric of Cape Cod.

Furthermore, the farm-to-table movement has influenced the craft beverage scene on Cape Cod, with many breweries and wineries incorporating locally sourced ingredients into their products. Some breweries experiment with flavors by incorporating locally grown fruits, herbs, and spices into their beer recipes, creating unique and seasonal offerings. Similarly, wineries may feature wines made from grapes that thrive in the coastal climate, resulting in wines with a distinctive Cape Cod character. This emphasis on local ingredients not only showcases the region's agricultural diversity but also strengthens the bond between craft beverage producers and local farmers, creating a symbiotic relationship that benefits the entire community.

For those looking to explore the Cape Cod craft beverage scene beyond individual breweries and wineries, guided tours and tasting experiences are available. These tours offer an opportunity to learn about the brewing and winemaking processes, as well as the history and stories behind each establishment. Whether it's a walking tour through the scenic vineyards, a behind-the-scenes look at the brewing equipment, or a guided tasting led by knowledgeable staff, these experiences provide a deeper understanding and appreciation for the craft and artistry behind each beverage.

Moreover, the craft beverage scene on Cape Cod goes beyond traditional beer and wine. The region is also home to cideries, meaderies, and distilleries that produce a range of unique and handcrafted libations. These establishments offer alternatives to beer and wine, showcasing the versatility and creativity of Cape Cod's craft beverage makers. From crisp and refreshing ciders made from local apples to honey-based meads and artisanal spirits, there is something for every palate to enjoy.

20

Shopping and Entertainment

Cape Cod, with its picturesque landscapes and charming coastal towns, offers a shopping experience that is as diverse and unique as the region itself. From quaint boutiques to bustling shopping centers, Cape Cod boasts an array of options for retail therapy. Join us as we embark on a journey through the vibrant shopping scene of Cape Cod, where visitors can find everything from local crafts and artisanal goods to high-end fashion and antique treasures.

One of the highlights of shopping on Cape Cod is the abundance of charming, independently owned boutiques and specialty shops that line the streets of its towns and villages. These hidden gems offer a curated selection of products, often reflecting the coastal and nautical themes that define the region's aesthetic.

Provincetown, known for its vibrant arts scene, is a treasure trove of unique shops and galleries. The town's Commercial Street is home to a myriad of boutiques where visitors can find local artwork, handmade jewelry, and one-of-a-kind fashion pieces. From contemporary art galleries to bohemian-inspired clothing stores, Provincetown's shopping scene is a haven for those seeking distinctive and creative finds.

Chatham, a quintessential Cape Cod town, also offers a delightful shopping experience. Main Street in Chatham is lined with charming boutiques that cater to a variety of tastes. From upscale clothing boutiques and home décor stores to gourmet food shops and artisanal gift boutiques, there is something for everyone. Visitors can browse through carefully curated collections of coastal-inspired fashion, unique home furnishings, and locally sourced gourmet treats, making Chatham a must-visit destination for those seeking a blend of sophistication and coastal charm.

For a more expansive shopping experience, Cape Cod has several shopping centers and malls that cater to a range of interests and budgets. The Cape Cod Mall in Hyannis is the region's largest shopping center, featuring a diverse selection of national retailers, department stores, and specialty shops. Here, shoppers can find everything from popular fashion brands to home goods, electronics, and beauty products. The mall also offers a variety of dining options, making it a convenient one-stop destination for shopping and entertainment.

In addition to boutique shopping and large shopping centers, Cape Cod is renowned for its vibrant art and craft scene. The region is home to numerous art galleries and studios where visitors can discover unique works of art created by local artists. From paintings and sculptures to pottery and jewelry, these art establishments showcase the talent and creativity that thrive in Cape Cod. Some galleries even offer the opportunity to meet the artists and gain insights into their creative process. Art lovers can explore the artistic enclaves of Provincetown, Wellfleet, and Falmouth (that we have discussed in earlier chapters), among others, to immerse themselves in the local art scene and bring home a piece of Cape Cod's creative spirit.

For those seeking antique treasures and vintage finds, Cape Cod is a paradise. The region boasts an array of antique shops and vintage boutiques that offer a glimpse into the past. From antique furniture and collectibles to vintage clothing and décor, these shops transport shoppers to bygone eras. Main Street in Sandwich is particularly known for its antique shops, where collectors and enthusiasts can uncover unique pieces and timeless treasures.

Cape Cod's shopping experience extends beyond traditional retail spaces. The region hosts a variety of vibrant farmers' markets, flea markets, and craft fairs that bring together local artisans, farmers, and purveyors. These markets offer an opportunity to browse and purchase locally sourced produce, handcrafted goods, and unique souvenirs. Farmers' markets, such as the one in Osterville and Wellfleet, showcase the region's agricultural bounty, including fresh fruits, vegetables, flowers, and artisanal products. Meanwhile, craft fairs, such as the Sandwich Artisans Fair and the Barnstable Village Crafts and Antiques Fair, provide a platform for local artisans to display their handmade creations, including jewelry, pottery, textiles, and woodworking. These markets and fairs not only offer a chance to support local producers and artisans but also provide a lively and interactive shopping experience where visitors can engage with the creators behind the products.

Furthermore, Cape Cod is home to several outlet malls and discount centers, offering shoppers the opportunity to snag great deals on popular brands. The Cape Cod Factory Outlet Mall in Sagamore features a variety of outlet stores, including clothing, footwear, and accessories, where shoppers can find discounted prices on their favorite brands. These outlets are particularly popular among bargain hunters and those looking to expand their wardrobes without breaking the bank.

Entertainment in Cape Cod

One of the highlights of entertainment in Cape Cod is its thriving performing arts scene. The region boasts a variety of theaters, concert venues, and music festivals that showcase a wide range of performances, from acclaimed Broadway shows to local theater productions and live music events.

The Cape Playhouse in Dennis, known as the "Birthplace of the Stars," has been a cultural hub since 1927. This historic theater hosts a summer season filled with Broadway-quality productions, featuring renowned actors and actresses who bring captivating performances to the stage. From classic plays and musicals to contemporary works, the Cape Playhouse offers a theater experience that rivals those found in major metropolitan areas.

Another notable venue is the Cape Cod Melody Tent in Hyannis. This unique, circular tent theater presents a diverse lineup of concerts and performances throughout the summer months.

With its intimate setting and revolving stage, the Melody Tent offers an immersive experience, allowing audiences to get up close and personal with their favorite artists. From renowned musicians and bands to comedy acts and children's shows, the Melody Tent caters to a wide range of musical tastes and entertainment preferences.

For those seeking a blend of art and entertainment, Cape Cod's art galleries and museums provide a visual feast for the senses. The Cape Cod Museum of Art in Dennis showcases a diverse collection of artwork by local and regional artists. Visitors can explore rotating exhibitions that span various artistic mediums, including paintings, sculptures, photography, and mixed media. The museum also hosts artist talks, workshops, and community events that foster creativity and engagement with the arts.

Additionally, Cape Cod's picturesque landscapes serve as inspiration for many artists, and visitors can often find open-air art shows and plein air painting events throughout the region. These events allow artists to showcase their work while capturing the beauty of Cape Cod's natural surroundings, creating a unique blend of entertainment and artistic expression.

Cape Cod is also a haven for music lovers, with numerous venues and festivals celebrating a wide range of musical genres. The Provincetown Jazz Festival, held annually in Provincetown, brings together world-class jazz musicians for a series of captivating performances. From smooth melodies to energetic improvisations, the festival showcases the richness and diversity of jazz music in an idyllic seaside setting.

In addition to live performances, Cape Cod offers an abundance of outdoor entertainment options. The region's pristine beaches provide the perfect backdrop for a day of relaxation, water sports, and beachside fun. Whether it's swimming, sunbathing, or building sandcastles with the family, the beach offers endless opportunities for enjoyment and entertainment.

Cape Cod's natural beauty extends beyond its beaches, offering breathtaking landscapes for outdoor enthusiasts to explore. The Cape Cod National Seashore, a 40-mile stretch of protected coastline, provides opportunities for hiking, biking, and nature walks amidst dunes, marshes, and forests. Visitors can immerse themselves in the region's natural wonders, spot diverse wildlife, and breathe in the fresh ocean air.

For those seeking adventure and thrill, Cape Cod offers a range of recreational activities such as kayaking, paddleboarding, and sailing. The region's calm bays and winding rivers provide ideal conditions for water-based activities, allowing visitors to enjoy the serenity of the water while engaging in exhilarating pursuits.

Cape Cod's family-friendly attractions are also a major source of entertainment. The Cape Cod Children's Museum in Mashpee offers interactive exhibits and hands-on activities designed to stimulate children's curiosity and creativity. From science experiments and building blocks to imaginative play areas and art workshops, the museum provides a fun and educational environment for young minds to explore and learn.

Another family favorite is the Cape Cod Inflatable Park in West Yarmouth. This outdoor amusement park features a variety of inflatable structures, including slides, obstacle courses, and bounce houses. Children can bounce, slide, and climb their way through the park, enjoying hours of active play and laughter.

Animal lovers will delight in the Cape Cod Zooquarium in West Yarmouth. This unique attraction combines a zoo and an aquarium, allowing visitors to get up close and personal with a wide array of animals from both land and sea. From lions and tigers to penguins and sharks, the Zooquarium offers an exciting and educational experience for visitors of all ages.

Cape Cod's rich maritime history is also celebrated through various entertainment offerings. The Cape Cod Maritime Museum in Hyannis showcases the region's seafaring heritage through exhibits, artifacts, and interactive displays. Visitors can learn about the importance of maritime industries, explore model ships, and even try their hand at navigating a simulated ship.

For a more immersive experience, visitors can embark on a scenic boat tour or a fishing excursion. These guided tours take visitors on a journey through Cape Cod's coastal waters, providing opportunities to spot marine life, learn about local ecosystems, and witness breathtaking views of the coastline. Whether it's a leisurely cruise, a whale watching adventure, or a deep-sea fishing expedition, these experiences offer a unique blend of entertainment and exploration.

Cape Cod's entertainment scene also extends to its vibrant festivals and community events. Throughout the year, the region hosts a variety of festivals that celebrate art, music, food, and local culture. The Cape Cod Scallop Fest in East Falmouth is a popular event that showcases the region's culinary delights, with fresh seafood dishes, live entertainment, and a festive atmosphere. The Cape Cod Hydrangea Festival, held annually in July, celebrates the iconic flower with garden tours, workshops, and special events that highlight the beauty of Cape Cod's landscapes.

VI

SOME PRACTICAL CONSIDERATIONS

21

Accommodation Options

As a first-time visitor or tourist, Cape Cod offers a wide range of accommodation options to suit every taste, budget, and preference. Whether you're seeking a luxurious beachfront resort, a cozy bed and breakfast, or a family-friendly vacation rental, Cape Cod's hospitality industry ensures that visitors have a comfortable and memorable stay. Join us as we explore the diverse accommodation choices available on Cape Cod.

Beachfront Resorts and Hotels:

For those seeking a luxurious and indulgent experience, Cape Cod is home to several beachfront resorts and hotels that offer stunning ocean views, upscale amenities, and a range of services designed to pamper guests. These resorts often feature private beach access, on-site dining options, spas, and recreational facilities such as pools, tennis courts, and golf courses. Whether you prefer the elegance of a grand resort or the intimacy of a boutique hotel, Cape Cod's beachfront accommodations provide a tranquil and idyllic setting for relaxation and rejuvenation.

Here are some beachfront hotels and resorts in Cape Cod that are suitable for tourists and first-time visitors:

1.Chatham Bars Inn (Chatham): This iconic luxury resort offers a stunning beachfront location, elegant accommodations, and a range of amenities including multiple dining options, a spa, and a private beach.

2. Wequassett Resort and Golf Club (Harwich): Situated on Pleasant Bay, Wequassett Resort offers luxurious rooms and suites, award-winning dining, a golf course, tennis courts, and access to a private beach.

3. Ocean Edge Resort & Golf Club (Brewster): This expansive resort boasts a breathtaking location on Cape Cod Bay, offering a variety of accommodations, multiple dining options, a golf course, pools, tennis courts, and access to a private beach.

4. Sea Crest Beach Hotel (North Falmouth): With its prime location on Old Silver Beach, Sea Crest Beach Hotel offers comfortable rooms, oceanfront dining, an outdoor pool, a private beach, and various activities such as paddleboarding and beach volleyball.

5. Red Jacket Beach Resort (South Yarmouth): Situated on a private beach overlooking Nantucket Sound, Red Jacket Beach Resort features cozy accommodations, on-site dining, a children's program, a heated pool, and access to a private beach.

6. The Mansion at Ocean Edge Resort & Golf Club (Brewster): This historic mansion offers luxury accommodations, an up-

scale restaurant, a spa, an outdoor pool, and access to a private beach on Cape Cod Bay.

7. The Provincetown Inn (Provincetown): Located on a picturesque stretch of beach, The Provincetown Inn offers comfortable rooms, waterfront dining, an outdoor pool, and beautiful views of Cape Cod Bay.

8. The Seacrest Beach Hotel (Falmouth): Situated directly on Old Silver Beach, The Seacrest Beach Hotel offers modern accommodations, a beachfront restaurant, an outdoor pool, and easy access to water sports and beach activities.

9. Sandbars Inn (North Truro): This charming inn overlooks Cape Cod Bay and offers comfortable accommodations with stunning ocean views, as well as a private beach and access to nearby hiking trails.

10. Cape Codder Resort & Spa (Hyannis): Though not directly on the beach, this family-friendly resort features an indoor wave pool, a spa, multiple dining options, and a convenient location near beaches and Hyannis attractions.

Charming Bed and Breakfasts:
   Cape Cod is known for its charming bed and breakfast establishments, which offer a personalized and cozy experience for visitors. These historic homes and inn-style accommodations often feature comfortable rooms, homemade breakfasts, and attentive hosts who provide local insights and recommendations. Bed and breakfasts are scattered throughout Cape Cod's towns and villages, allowing visitors to immerse themselves in

the region's unique culture and hospitality. From Victorian-era mansions to quaint cottages, these accommodations provide a warm and welcoming atmosphere that captures the essence of Cape Cod.

Here are some bed and breakfasts in Cape Cod that are suitable for tourists and first-time visitors:

1.Captain's House Inn (Chatham): This elegant B&B offers luxurious rooms and suites in a beautifully restored 19th-century captain's mansion. Guests can enjoy a gourmet breakfast, afternoon tea, and access to amenities such as a pool and tennis courts.

2. The Platinum Pebble Boutique Inn (West Harwich): This boutique inn offers modern and stylish accommodations, gourmet breakfast, complimentary bikes for exploring the area, and a convenient location near beaches and attractions.

3. Ashley Manor (Barnstable): Located in the historic district of Barnstable Village, Ashley Manor is a charming B&B housed in a restored 17th-century home. Guests can relax in beautifully appointed rooms and enjoy a delicious breakfast each morning.

4. Isaiah Jones Homestead (Sandwich): Set in a historic Victorian mansion, Isaiah Jones Homestead offers comfortable and spacious rooms, a delicious homemade breakfast, and a peaceful garden for relaxation.

5. The Palmer House Inn (Falmouth): This romantic inn is housed in a charming Victorian mansion and offers individu-

ally decorated rooms, a delicious breakfast, and a convenient location near Falmouth's shops and restaurants.

6. Inn on the Beach (Harwich): As the name suggests, this B&B offers beachfront accommodations with stunning ocean views. Guests can enjoy direct access to the beach, cozy rooms, a delicious breakfast, and a warm and welcoming atmosphere.

7. Candleberry Inn on Cape Cod (Brewster): This historic inn offers beautifully decorated rooms, a gourmet breakfast, and a convenient location near Brewster's beaches, bike trails, and attractions.

8. The Captain Farris House (South Yarmouth): Located in a charming village, this inn offers comfortable rooms, a hearty breakfast, and a peaceful garden for relaxation. Guests can also enjoy proximity to the beach and Cape Cod's attractions.

9. The Inn at Cape Cod (Yarmouth Port): Set in a classic Cape Cod-style mansion, this B&B offers elegant rooms, a gourmet breakfast, and a peaceful atmosphere. Guests can also enjoy the inn's beautiful gardens and convenient location.

10. Sea Meadow Inn (Brewster): This tranquil inn offers comfortable accommodations, a gourmet breakfast, and a serene garden setting. It is conveniently located near Brewster's beaches and attractions.

These are just a few examples of bed and breakfasts in Cape Cod that cater to tourists and first-time visitors. Each offers its own unique charm, hospitality, and amenities, providing a cozy and memorable stay on Cape Cod.

Vacation Rentals and Cottages:

For those looking for a home away from home experience, Cape Cod offers a plethora of vacation rentals and cottages that provide privacy and flexibility. These fully furnished properties range from cozy cottages to spacious beach houses, allowing families and larger groups to enjoy ample space and the convenience of a kitchen and living area. Vacation rentals often come equipped with amenities such as outdoor grills, decks or patios, and even access to private beaches or pools. Renting a vacation home or cottage gives visitors the freedom to create their own schedule and enjoy a more personalized and independent stay.

Quaint Inns and Motels:

Cape Cod is dotted with quaint inns and motels that cater to a variety of budgets. These accommodations offer a comfortable and affordable option for travelers who are looking for a convenient place to rest and explore the region. Inns and motels often feature clean and cozy rooms, complimentary breakfast, and friendly staff who can provide local recommendations and assistance. While they may not offer the same extensive amenities as larger resorts, these accommodations provide a cost-effective option for those who plan to spend most of their time exploring Cape Cod's attractions and natural beauty.

Campgrounds and RV Parks:

For outdoor enthusiasts and nature lovers, Cape Cod's campgrounds and RV parks provide a unique accommodation option. These locations allow visitors to immerse themselves in the region's natural beauty while enjoying the comfort of their own camping equipment or recreational vehicle. Cape Cod offers several campgrounds with varying amenities, including access to hiking trails, swimming ponds, and picnic areas. Whether you prefer pitching a tent under the stars or parking your RV in a scenic setting, camping on Cape Cod offers a rustic and adventurous experience.

Accessible Accommodations:

Cape Cod also caters to visitors with specific accessibility needs. Many hotels, resorts, and vacation rentals offer accessible rooms and facilities, ensuring that all guests can enjoy a comfortable and inclusive stay. These accommodations may feature accessible entrances, roll-in showers, and other amenities designed to accommodate individuals with disabilities. Additionally, Cape Cod offers various accessible attractions and services, including wheelchair-accessible beaches, accessible transportation options, and guided tours that cater to individuals with mobility challenges.

Regardless of the type of accommodation chosen, first-time visitors and tourists to Cape Cod can expect warm and welcoming hospitality, along with a range of amenities and services to enhance their stay. Many accommodations offer additional features such as complimentary breakfast, Wi-Fi access, on-site parking, and concierge services to ensure a seamless and enjoyable experience.

Cape Cod's accommodations not only provide a comfortable place to rest but also serve as a gateway to the region's attractions and activities. Many hotels and resorts offer packages and deals that include access to nearby beaches, golf courses, water sports, and other recreational opportunities. Some accommodations even provide bike rentals or shuttle services, making it convenient for guests to explore the charming towns and scenic routes of Cape Cod.

Location is another important consideration when choosing accommodation on Cape Cod. Visitors can opt to stay in the heart of bustling towns like Provincetown, Hyannis, or Chatham, where they will find a vibrant atmosphere, lively entertainment, and a wide array of dining options. Alternatively, those seeking a quieter and more secluded retreat may choose accommodations in the charming villages and rural areas of Cape Cod, where they can immerse themselves in the region's natural beauty and tranquility.

It's worth noting that Cape Cod's popularity as a tourist destination means that accommodations can book up quickly during peak seasons, especially in the summer months. Therefore, it is advisable to plan and book in advance to secure the desired accommodation and dates.

For visitors looking to make the most of their Cape Cod experience, it's also beneficial to consider the proximity of accommodation to the region's top attractions. Whether it's exploring the historic sites of Plymouth, visiting the Cape Cod National Seashore, or embarking on a whale-watching excursion, choosing accommodation that offers easy access to these attractions can save time and enhance the overall experience.

22

Practical Information

Weather and Best Time to Visit
Cape Cod, with its picturesque beaches, charming towns, and natural beauty, attracts visitors year-round. To make the most of your trip, it's important to understand the weather patterns and determine the best time to visit based on your preferences and desired activities. Here, we will discuss the weather in Cape Cod and provide guidance on the best time to plan your visit.

Cape Cod experiences a varied climate throughout the year, influenced by its coastal location. Summers are generally warm and pleasant, while winters tend to be cold and snowy. Spring and fall bring milder temperatures and colorful foliage, making them popular seasons for outdoor activities and exploration.

Summer (June to August):
Summer is the peak tourist season in Cape Cod, attracting visitors with its sunny days and warm temperatures. Average highs range from the mid-70s to low 80s Fahrenheit (24-29

degrees Celsius), making it ideal for beach activities, swimming, and outdoor adventures. July and August are the busiest months, with vibrant festivals, bustling towns, and lively nightlife. However, it's important to note that summer can also bring occasional humidity and crowded beaches. Advanced bookings for accommodation and popular attractions are recommended during this time.

Fall (September to November):

Fall in Cape Cod offers mild temperatures and stunning foliage as the region transforms into a kaleidoscope of colors. September and October are particularly beautiful, with average highs ranging from the 60s to 70s Fahrenheit (15-25 degrees Celsius). It's a great time to explore nature trails, go biking, or visit local farms for apple and pumpkin picking. Fall also brings fewer crowds, making it a more peaceful and relaxed time to enjoy the region's attractions.

Winter (December to February):

Cape Cod experiences cold and snowy winters, with average temperatures ranging from the 30s to 40s Fahrenheit (0-5 degrees Celsius). While the beaches may not be suitable for swimming during this time, winter offers a unique charm with fewer tourists and a quieter atmosphere. It's an excellent season for cozying up in front of a fireplace, exploring historic sites, enjoying winter sports like ice skating, and experiencing the region's festive holiday events.

Spring (March to May):

Spring brings the awakening of nature in Cape Cod, with blooming flowers, migrating birds, and a fresh sense of renewal. Average temperatures in spring range from the 40s to 60s Fahrenheit (5-20 degrees Celsius). It's an excellent time for birdwatching, exploring nature reserves, and enjoying the serenity of the region before the summer crowds arrive. Spring also offers the opportunity to witness the Cape's fishing industry in action and indulge in delicious local seafood.

When deciding the best time to visit Cape Cod, consider your interests, preferred activities, and tolerance for crowds. If you're seeking a lively and vibrant atmosphere with a plethora of events and activities, summer is the prime time. However, if you prefer a quieter experience with milder temperatures and scenic beauty, spring and fall are ideal. Winter appeals to those who enjoy a peaceful getaway, winter sports, and festive holiday celebrations.

It's important to note that weather conditions can vary, and it's always wise to check the forecast before your trip. Cape Cod's coastal location means that temperatures can be influenced by ocean breezes, and conditions may change rapidly. Layered clothing and packing essentials like sunscreen, hats, and insect repellent are recommended, regardless of the season.

Safety Tips

While Cape Cod offers a welcoming and safe environment, it's always important to prioritize your safety and well-being during your visit. Whether you're exploring the coastline, engaging in outdoor adventures, or simply enjoying the local attractions, following these safety tips will ensure a secure and enjoyable experience.

1. Swim Safely: Cape Cod's beautiful beaches are a major attraction, but it's crucial to be aware of water safety. Swim only in designated swimming areas with lifeguards present. Pay attention to warning flags, currents, and tides. If you're not a strong swimmer, consider wearing a life jacket or using flotation devices. Supervise children closely and never leave them unattended near the water.

2. Be Sun Smart: Cape Cod's sunny climate calls for proper sun protection. Wear sunscreen with a high SPF, even on cloudy days, and reapply it regularly. Protect your eyes with sunglasses and wear a wide-brimmed hat to shield your face from the sun. Seek shade during peak sun hours and stay hydrated by drinking plenty of water.

3. Stay Hydrated: Cape Cod's outdoor activities and warm temperatures can lead to dehydration. Carry a reusable water bottle and drink plenty of fluids throughout the day. Avoid excessive consumption of alcohol and caffeinated beverages, as they can contribute to dehydration.

4. Practice Wildlife Safety: Cape Cod is home to various wildlife, including seals, birds, and marine creatures. While observing wildlife can be exciting, it's important to maintain a safe distance and avoid disturbing or feeding them. Admire wildlife from a distance, respect their habitats, and follow any guidelines or regulations provided by park authorities.

5. Be Mindful of Weather Conditions: Cape Cod's weather can be unpredictable, so it's essential to stay informed about current and forecasted conditions. Check the weather forecast before

heading out and be prepared for changes in temperature, wind, and precipitation. Dress appropriately for the weather and bring necessary gear such as rain jackets, extra layers, or sun protection.

6. Stay on Designated Trails: Cape Cod offers numerous hiking and biking trails that allow visitors to explore its natural beauty. Stick to designated paths and trails to avoid getting lost or damaging sensitive ecosystems. Be cautious of uneven terrain, slippery surfaces, and wildlife encounters. Carry a map, stay aware of your surroundings, and inform someone about your intended route and estimated return time.

7. Secure Your Belongings: Cape Cod is generally a safe destination, but it's always wise to take precautions to protect your belongings. Keep valuables and important documents secure in your accommodation or use a hotel safe if available. When out and about, never leave personal items unattended and be mindful of your surroundings in crowded places.

8. Respect the Environment: Cape Cod's natural beauty relies on responsible tourism and sustainable practices. Preserve the region's pristine beaches and coastal ecosystems by practicing Leave No Trace principles. Dispose of trash properly, avoid littering, and respect signage and regulations in protected areas.

9. Follow Traffic Rules: If you're driving in Cape Cod, familiarize yourself with local traffic rules and regulations. Observe speed limits, wear seat belts, and avoid distractions while driving. Be cautious of pedestrians and cyclists, particularly in busy areas.

10. Seek Local Knowledge: Take advantage of the local knowledge and resources available in Cape Cod. Consult with park rangers, visitor centers, or knowledgeable locals for information on specific activities, safety guidelines, and current conditions. They can provide valuable insights and recommendations to enhance your experience while keeping you safe.

By following these safety tips, you can ensure a secure and enjoyable visit to Cape Cod. Remember, your well being and safety should always be a top priority. Here are a few additional safety tips to keep in mind:

Plan Ahead: Before embarking on any outdoor activities or excursions, it's essential to plan ahead. Research the area, familiarize yourself with the terrain, and understand any potential risks or hazards associated with your chosen activities. Check for any advisories, closures, or restrictions in the region.

Use Caution in Water Activities: If you're planning to engage in water activities such as kayaking, paddleboarding, or boating, ensure you have the necessary skills and experience. Wear appropriate safety gear, such as life jackets or personal flotation devices. Check weather conditions and tides before heading out and let someone know your plans and expected return time.

Stay Connected: It's advisable to carry a fully charged cell phone with you at all times. In case of an emergency or if you need assistance, having a means of communication can be crucial. Save important phone numbers, including emergency contacts and local authorities, in your phone.

Essential Contacts

When visiting Cape Cod, it's important to have a list of essential contacts readily available to ensure your safety and convenience during your stay. Here are some essential contacts that you should keep on hand:

Emergency Services:

Emergency: 911

In case of a life-threatening emergency, contact 911 for immediate assistance from police, fire, or medical services.

Local Authorities:

Cape Cod Police Department: Contact the local police department for non-emergency situations or to report incidents that require police attention. The specific contact details may vary depending on the town you are in, so it's advisable to find the local police department's contact information for your location.

Medical Services:

Local Hospitals/Clinics: Find the contact information for nearby hospitals or clinics in Cape Cod. Inquire about their emergency services and availability.

Poison Control:

If you require assistance or information regarding poisoning or exposure to harmful substances, contact the Poison Control Center at the appropriate number for your location.

Transportation:

Local Taxi Services: Keep the contact information for local taxi services in Cape Cod. Taxis can be useful for transportation within towns or for travel to and from the airport or other destinations.

Car Rental Agencies:

If you plan to rent a car during your visit, have the contact details for car rental agencies available.

Accommodation:

Hotel/Accommodation Reception: Save the contact information for the reception desk or front desk of your accommodation. They can provide assistance with any questions or concerns you may have during your stay.

Tourist Information:

Local Visitor Centers: Note the contact information for tourist information centers or visitor centers in Cape Cod. They can provide valuable assistance, including maps, brochures, and recommendations for local attractions and activities.

Consular Services:

Embassy/Consulate: If you are a foreign visitor, note the contact details of your country's embassy or consulate in case of any consular services required during your stay.

Airlines:

Airline Customer Service: Save the contact information for your airline's customer service in case you need to make changes to your flight or have any inquiries or issues related to your air travel.

Credit Card Companies:

Credit Card Customer Service: Keep the contact information for your credit card companies readily available in case of any problems, such as lost or stolen cards, fraudulent charges, or billing inquiries.

Local Tourism Helpline:

Cape Cod Tourism Helpline: Check if there is a local tourism helpline or information hotline specific to Cape Cod. This helpline can assist with general inquiries, recommendations, and any concerns related to your visit.

Remember to save these essential contacts in your phone or have them written down in case of emergencies or when you need assistance or information. It's always better to be prepared and have access to the necessary contacts during your time in Cape Cod.

VII

Conclusion

As we come to the end of our journey through Cape Cod, it becomes evident that this picturesque peninsula is an extraordinary destination that offers something for everyone. From pristine beaches to charming towns, from outdoor adventures to cultural experiences, Cape Cod truly has it all.